FAQs on OCD

Ashley Fulwood and Zoë Wilson

Written by people with lived experience of OCD,
for people living with OCD

All author royalties from this book will benefit
the national charity OCD-UK

sheldon PRESS

First published in Great Britain by Sheldon Press in 2022
An imprint of John Murray Press
A division of Hodder & Stoughton Ltd,
An Hachette UK company

2

This book is for information or educational purposes only and is
not intended to act as a substitute for medical advice or treatment.
Any person with a condition requiring medical attention should
consult a qualified medical practitioner or suitable therapist.

A CIP catalogue record for this title is available from the British Library

Trade Paperback ISBN 978 1 399 80268 0
eBook ISBN 978 1 399 80269 7

Typeset in Caecilia LT Std by
Palimpsest Book Production Ltd, Falkirk, Stirlingshire

Printed and bound in Great Britain by Clays Ltd, Elcograf S.p.A.

John Murray Press policy is to use papers that are natural, renewable
and recyclable products and made from wood grown in sustainable
forests. The logging and manufacturing processes are expected to
conform to the environmental regulations of the country of origin.

John Murray Press
Carmelite House
50 Victoria Embankment
London EC4Y 0DZ

www.sheldonpress.co.uk

Dedicated to all those courageous people living with
Obsessive-Compulsive Disorder, who daily courto face
and survive OCD challenges remain inspiration to us,
and why we felt it was important write this book.

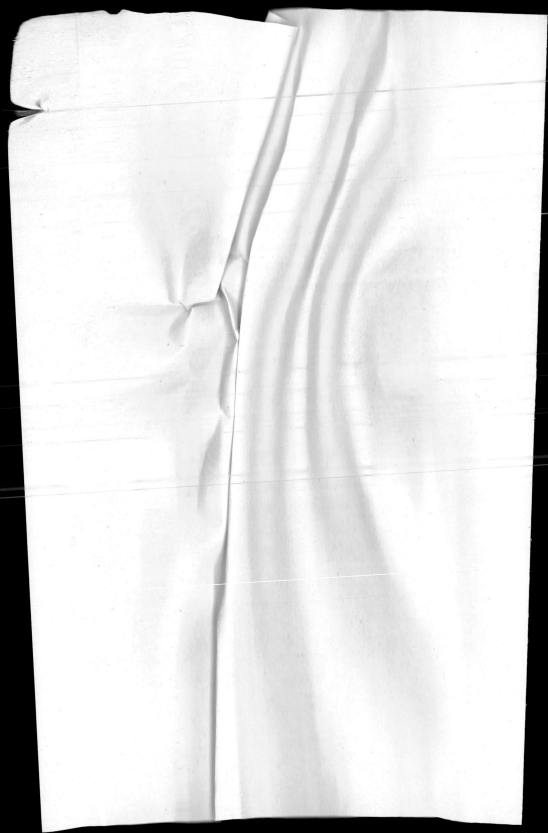

Contents

Foreword   vii

Introduction   xi

Preface   xiii

1 About OCD – The Basics   1

2 Understanding OCD   12

3 Debunking OCD Myths   27

4 Children and OCD   37

5 Lifestyle   50

6 Diagnosing OCD   58

7 Treatment for OCD   62

8 How to Access Treatment   74

9 Treatment Myths   81

10 OCD Self-help   87

11 Working and OCD   92

12 Life in Recovery   99

FAQs list   106

About the Authors   110

Acknowledgements   112

Foreword

What a great book and what a privilege to introduce it to you. Ashley, Zoe and I agree on many things. Perhaps foremost of these is the fact that Obsessive Compulsive Disorder (OCD) is an unnecessary illness. By this, we mean that, given the right help, guidance and support, it is possible for those affected to take back their lives from OCD. In the worst case, people can still be left with the problems which OCD has caused, sometimes called 'collateral damage', where years of struggling with OCD has robbed the affected person (and often their loved ones too) of life opportunities. We know that the time between developing OCD to it being correctly identified typically is an average of 10 years, and getting effective treatment is much longer than that. I do not want to dwell on the shameful extent of inadequate and inappropriate treatment offered to sufferers, but it is commonplace and of course typically makes things worse. What, then, can be done? Actually, quite a lot, and you could do worse to start with this gem of a book.

As you will learn in this book, the problem with OCD is that some people become trapped or stuck in particular ways of reacting to what for most are normal intrusive thoughts, images, impulses and doubts. Those who develop OCD become concerned not only about the harm which such intrusions suggest is possible, but also about the possibility of their being responsible for it. This leads to attempts to control intrusions and the harm suggested by them, which has the opposite effect to that intended. Sufferers also put huge efforts into trying to make sure that they are not responsible for any harm to themselves and/or other people. Simply put, in OCD the solution becomes the problem. Attempts to manage intrusions become all-consuming; rituals such as washing and checking take more and more time and strengthen the original fears, and the person lives on what can feel like a permanent knife-edge. OCD becomes a self-reinforcing trap, because it is fundamentally a problem of trying too hard, which makes things worse. People with OCD try too hard to get rid of unwanted intrusions, to be sure that they have checked enough, and so on. The harder you try to do these things, the more concerned you become.

To escape this trap, a crucial first step is to know OCD for what it is and realise that it has many pernicious faces which promise relief but deliver torture. "Just one more check and I will feel sure...". This book helps the reader to begin to understand how OCD really works, clearly and with the voice of those who have reached an understanding of the problem and can help you and your loved ones begin to understand as well. The next step is to take back control and reclaim your life. Zoe and Ashley are quite clear that this is far from easy, but also that it is entirely possible. Their writing reflects what we know from many years of research, which is that Cognitive Behaviour Therapy (CBT), which includes both behavioural experiments and Exposure and Response Prevention, is what is needed. Most people regard CBT as something done by therapists as 'treatment'. As Ashley and Zoe make clear, this is not so; they say, 'The principal aim of CBT is to provide us with the tools and knowledge to become our own therapists, and practise what we know persistently so we are able to work towards recovery from Obsessive-Compulsive Disorder'.

From many years of working to understand and help those with OCD, it has become clear to me that what happens on the road to recovery is that, if the sufferer understands how OCD works (and how it tricks them into sustaining it), they can test out this new understanding by beginning to break the rules set by their OCD. Ashley and I have several times discussed the factor we think represents the turning point for many of those working to beat their OCD, which is the point at which they 'choose to change'. Choosing to change is different from being pushed, cajoled or coerced into stopping rituals, because it represents the person with OCD actively taking charge. To actively challenge your OCD means that you are considering a different, less threatening way of understanding yourself, and your world. The person who compulsively washes can consider that, rather than being dangerously contaminated, they are a clean person who is afraid of being dirty. The person who checks excessively may move from the idea that their behaviour is risky to the alternative that they are actually a careful person who is afraid of causing harm.

Successful treatment for OCD comes from the person as they expose the cruel lies that OCD tells them and begin to experiment with different ways of dealing with and overcoming their fears. Having support in these efforts from your loved ones, support groups and organizations and professionals can be helpful, of course, but ultimately the impetus comes from you as you undertake the journey to improvement and recovery. This fantastic book will help you on that journey.

Professor Paul Salkovskis, PhD, FBPsS,
Honorary Fellow of the BABCP

Oxford Health NHS Foundation Trust and
University of Oxford Centre for Psychological Health

Introduction

Having both experienced and suffered from Obsessive-Compulsive Disorder (OCD), we know all too well the pain and devastation this insidious condition brings. We recognize that nagging angst and those unrelenting intrusive thoughts that cause so much anguish and guilt. We know that feeling that something isn't quite right and the unwavering urge to carry out a behaviour just one more time, before we loop back and do it all again. We understand it takes great bravery and courage to live with OCD every day.

We recognize that each morning when you open your eyes, you often do so with the dread of knowing the torture OCD will bring, yet despite this face the challenge of having to get up and somehow navigate a day alongside triggers and intrusive thoughts that bombard us. OCD ensures that more often not, we can't live the life we choose to, and the decisions we make never feel like our own.

The internet places a lot of information at our fingertips about OCD, and OCD charity websites have a wealth of helpful information about the disorder. However, we know that sometimes people can feel overwhelmed with too much information all at once. People are often bombarded with copious amounts of literature which can be confusing, albeit offered with the best intention. Therefore, we have created a book with information in small, bite-sized chunks.

Living with this disorder often doesn't allow for long periods of respite from intrusive thoughts and distractions. Because of this, we wanted to create a resource which replaces hours of endless searching for answers and offers the opportunity to dip in and out of this book as and when you wish to in the weeks and months ahead.

Through our work with OCD-UK we have seen that often the practicalities of life with OCD are not always addressed or discussed. For many people, their reluctance to ask questions is fuelled by the fear of other people's reactions, fear of judgement, and how they may be perceived. This book aims to take all of that away from you, by asking and answering those questions which you may have wanted to ask for some time but have been reluctant to.

We promise you that no question is too embarrassing, naive, simple or complex to ask. In this FAQs book we will help you to navigate through some of the challenges that come with living with OCD, and the difficulties that can occur when working towards recovery. We will cover information on understanding what OCD is and how to access treatment, right through to the honest practicalities of living with OCD and dealing with the day-to-day challenges that are rarely talked about.

We hope that this book will not only be your companion along the difficult road of life with OCD, but also be your honest and trustworthy guide in your steps towards recovery, until one day it sits on your bookshelf gathering dust, watching you thrive as you live life your way, dictated by you, not Obsessive-Compulsive Disorder.

 Disclaimer

We encourage you to talk to your GP or mental health professional about your own mental health diagnosis and/or treatment.

The information in this book is correct at the time of going to print, however should there be any change we will update it via the national charity website of OCD-UK and in any subsequent versions of the book that we author.

Preface

Can I recover, or will I always have OCD?

Throughout this book we are going to be talking all things OCD, but we want to start with something important, and you could argue this is the most important question of all. Can you recover from OCD? The answer is: absolutely.

The reason why we are starting with this specific question is because we wanted to begin this book with a message of hope. If you have spent a long-time battling OCD, you will know what it's like to question if it's possible to take back control of your own life. It can be so hard to envision what recovery would even feel like, or what your days might look like when you have extra time for yourself, instead of carrying out hours' worth of exhausting and distressing compulsions.

If you are reading this as a loved one of someone who is suffering from OCD, you will know the constant worry and endless wondering about whether life will ever become easier for your loved one. You will know what it feels like to watch someone you care so deeply for be the target of a gruelling and complex mental health condition. But the truth is, a better life does exist, recovery is no myth and we all deserve to experience it. All of us. Those who are suffering, and those who love someone who is.

Recovery means something different to everyone of course, and it's important we respect how people personally feel about recovery. For one person it might mean no longer performing any compulsions at all, whereas for another it might mean despite the occasional setbacks here and there, the overall quality of their life has increased, and OCD is no longer in control of their day-to-day activities or responsibilities. Whatever recovery means to you, the reader, that's up for you to decide. I (Zoë) will be concluding this book by sharing what recovery means to me, personally, and Ashley will be sharing what it means to him.

Regardless of the little details, recovery means increased happiness, reduced distress and taking back control of your own life. This is completely possible, and knowing that it's possible might just be enough to help us grasp onto the hope we need to motivate us to keep challenging OCD.

If you are yet to start your recovery journey or feel like you have hit a brick wall with no tools to help you over it, just remember it's normal to wonder if recovery will ever happen for you. But recovery can and does happen, and there is no reason why you would be an exception. Small steps work towards big progress, and just because you don't have the tools to help you over the wall right now, it doesn't mean you won't find them.

We have to believe in recovery to be able to achieve it.

➤ The importance of self-compassion

Dealing with all of the negative emotions and feelings that OCD causes is hard enough without having to deal with the horrible things we can sometimes tell ourselves too. 'I am useless, I am weak, I have let everyone down, I have let myself down'. We both know all too well that feeling of disappointment when you've struggled to stand up to the OCD and it's taken charge of a situation, despite how much you wanted to challenge it and not let it win. We know how hard you can be on yourself when you know what actions you need to take to face the OCD beast, but you can't quite take that plunge.

It can also be really hard to be kind to yourself when OCD is trying to convince you that you are a disgusting, terrible and careless person. For some people, OCD has convinced them they don't deserve recovery at all. The condition has attacked their character to the point where they feel they don't deserve good things to happen to them. Who wouldn't experience low self-esteem when experiencing these intense feelings?

It's only natural to feel disappointed when OCD has won a battle, and it can sadly add to those feelings of low self-esteem. However, self-compassion is important in these situations. When we are compassionate with ourselves, we are reminding ourselves that it isn't our fault that we have this mental health problem. We are supporting ourselves to pick ourselves up, dust ourselves down and try again. Self-compassion is a reminder that now more than ever is a time that we need some kindness to get us through.

Throughout this book we will talk about recovery, how to challenge OCD, and the pathways we need to navigate down to reach recovery. However, what we want you to know is that if you are struggling to challenge OCD, or you are not yet at the goal you want to be at, that's OK. We have been there, we don't judge you and you aren't a failure. Be kind to yourself and keep putting one step in front of the other. You are worthy of gentleness and love, and most importantly, you are worthy of recovery.

About OCD – The Basics

Welcome to the first chapter of our book. You may already have some knowledge about OCD and how it works, but equally this could be the first time you are reading a book about OCD. Regardless of where you are with your understanding, we hope this chapter will offer something for everyone. We will cover what OCD is and some of the most commonly asked questions about the disorder itself.

Although many of the questions in this chapter you will read in other OCD literature, it's important we start with the basics because it's the foundation to everything else we explore in the book. Understanding every aspect of OCD puts us one step ahead in our quest to work towards recovery from Obsessive-Compulsive Disorder.

What is OCD?

Obsessive-Compulsive Disorder (routinely referred to as OCD) is an anxiety-related condition where a person experiences frequent intrusive and unwelcome obsessional thoughts, which leads to the person feeling compelled to carry out compulsive behaviours.

There are two significant aspects to OCD: obsessions, and compulsions (as the name suggests). The process of how our thoughts (obsessions) and our behaviours (compulsions) are entwined is quite complex. However, it's important we understand how it works, so we will explore this throughout this chapter.

No two people that suffer from OCD are alike. The thoughts and behaviours associated with OCD can vary in both theme and severity for each individual, both fluctuating over time. OCD is a very distressing condition which significantly interferes with a person's life. This is why it's important we highlight that the **D** in OC**D** stands for **disorder**.

What is an obsession?

The word 'obsession' can have a very different, and more trivial, meaning when used outside the context of OCD. In OCD, the word 'obsession' means the fear or worry a person is experiencing. Obsessions take the form of persistent, unwanted and uncontrollable intrusive thoughts or persistent images that pop into a person's head. They can be intense feelings and doubts, or sometimes a combination of all of these.

Intrusive thoughts in OCD are always unwanted, intrusive, and always very distressing in content and incredibly difficult to ignore. Most significantly, they interfere with the sufferer's ability to function on a day-to-day basis, which is why OCD is a disorder.

Before we go into a more complex explanation about obsessions in OCD, let's look at what most people think about the word 'obsession' and the different types of intrusive thoughts that everybody experiences. Many people at different stages of their life will have reoccurring thoughts which bring pleasure about something of interest, for example a band, actor or sports team. That object of interest may even become an obsession because the subject is followed with great passion. However, unlike with Obsessive-Compulsive Disorder, that obsession will be welcomed, pleasurable and bring some level of enjoyment, certainly initially.

When people with OCD experience obsessions their thoughts are triggered involuntarily and become focused on something non-pleasurable, negative and often about something bad, even catastrophic, happening to themselves or loved ones. It's for this reason that the obsessions in OCD become so distressing and will generate fear, worry, anguish and anxiety to the point where they begin to take over every moment. It can feel like a person's brain becomes locked as people are often unable to focus on anything else. This distress can make a person feel compelled to stop the thoughts through actions and behaviours.

The obsessions in OCD should not be confused with the compulsions; the obsession is the thought/fear/worry and the compulsions, as we will look at later, are the actions and behaviours carried out in attempt to stop the obsessions.

Several examples of **obsessions** in OCD are:

- feeling that things don't quite feel right

- worrying about catching media-publicized illnesses, such as HIV, COVID-19, bird flu or swine flu, and that you will pass that onto a loved one who will get badly ill or die

- worrying about causing physical or sexual harm to yourself or others

- unwanted and unpleasant sexual thoughts and feelings about sexuality or the fear of acting inappropriately towards children

- worrying that something terrible will happen

- fear of something bad happening unless checked (i.e. property will be broken into/will burn down)

- worrying that you have caused an accident whilst driving

- fears or feelings around being a disgusting person for having a specific thought, or for not washing after coming into contact with something considered disgusting (i.e. semen, blood, urine and any other bodily fluids)

- having the unpleasant feeling that you are about to shout out obscenities in public

This list of obsessions is by no means an exhaustive.

To sufferers and non-sufferers alike, the thoughts and fears related to OCD can often seem profoundly shocking, especially if they are of graphic or violent nature. It must be stressed that the thoughts do not precede intent, they are just thoughts which are not voluntarily produced.

It's perhaps worth mentioning that evidence shows us that intrusive thoughts are quite common in the general population, not just for those who suffer with OCD. Researchers have shown that the vast majority of people (in a general population) reported unwanted intrusive thoughts with content that is often identical to that of obsessions found in OCD.

It's important to remember that it's not the thought itself that is the problem, but the way people with OCD interpret – or rather misinterpret – and respond to the thought, which we will explore more later. It's this principle that should form part of good clinical treatment if we are to break free from OCD.

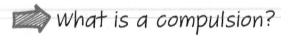 What is a compulsion?

A compulsion is any action or behaviour that a person feels compelled to carry out in response to distressing intrusive thoughts (obsessions), and the feelings and emotions they generate. The compulsions are intended to neutralize anxiety, achieve complete certainty or stop something 'bad' from happening.

The problem is, although the intention of the compulsion is to neutralize anxiety, any feelings of relief are always very short-lived. Some people don't experience any relief at all, and the compulsion itself creates even more uncertainty and anxiety.

Compulsions can be either specific physical actions, such as repeatedly checking a gas stove is off, or they can be silent mental checks, for example repeating words and phrases or going over past events in your mind to become certain about a particular incident or event, sometimes from the same day or from decades ago.

Reassurance-seeking and avoidance are also behaviours that fall into the category of compulsions. A person might try to achieve certainty by repeatedly asking other people questions like 'did I upset or hurt you?' or 'are you sure this surface isn't contaminated?' A person might also avoid certain people, object or places in the attempt to avoid something catastrophic. For example, avoiding knives because they are experiencing intrusive thoughts about harming someone. People might also avoid the news in case there are any reports or stories which trigger their intrusive thoughts.

OCD can lead to behaviours (compulsions) focused on any theme, but the following are some of the more common compulsions we might see in OCD and what might drive a person to carry them out:

- checking switches, cars, doors, taps, or locks – the obsessive thought might be to prevent danger from a fire/break-in

- mental compulsions, like counting or checking, to attempt to 'neutralize' an obsessional thought – the obsessive thought might be that something bad may happen if not carried out

- excessive washing of hands or body – the obsessive thought might be a fear of being contaminated or contaminating a loved one, which might cause harm/illness

- avoiding particular places, people or situations – the obsessive thought might be about harming someone or fears that people or places are contaminated

- checking the body – depending on the worry this could be looking for signs of an illness, or for arousal if OCD makes someone question their sexual orientation, or if they are attracted to someone inappropriate

- avoidance of kitchen knives and other such instruments, for example locking them in a drawer – the obsessive thought might be that a person fears they will stab a loved one inadvertently

- doing tasks deliberately slowly – this could be to make sure a task is done 'just right' or because the behaviour is done in such a rigid way, it needs to be repeated time and time again until the routine is done to perfection

- struggling to discard seemingly useless objects for either specific obsessive reasons, or because they have a 'feeling' they need to keep them to prevent something catastrophic from happening

Please don't worry if the compulsions that you carry out are not listed here – these are only the most common examples.

In summary, a compulsion can be any action or behaviour that a person feels compelled to carry out to prevent something bad from happening, in order to achieve complete certainty, and to neutralize the distressing intrusive thoughts (obsessions).

What is an OCD trigger?

Regardless of the symptoms a person with OCD may be suffering with, one thing everybody with OCD will be familiar with in one form or another is a 'trigger'. A trigger is anything that generates an intrusive thought and begins the OCD cycle process. It could be a place, person, physical object, a feeling of discomfort or an internal mental thought.

For example, if a person who is experiencing contamination-related fears needs to use the toilet whilst out in public, this event could trigger the intrusive thought 'the toilet is contaminated'. In another example, if a person who is experiencing harm-related fears, and someone comes up to them as they are using a knife in the kitchen, this could trigger the intrusive thought 'what if I harm someone with this knife?'

In both of these examples, it's not uncommon for someone with OCD to go to great lengths to 'avoid' their triggers to prevent hours of anguish. In the examples above, the individuals would avoid knives or areas that are perceived to be contaminated at all costs.

In summary, a trigger is the original source of the initial intrusive thought that begins the OCD cycle process.

 Why is OCD a disorder?

According to the *Oxford English Dictionary*, the word 'disorder' means 'an illness that disrupts normal physical or mental functions'. They can take up a lot of time and complicate the normal functioning of an individual, and it's fair to say that Obsessive-Compulsive Disorder ticks all those criteria.

Despite the severity of Obsessive-Compulsive Disorder, over the last decade we've seen the OCD acronym and 'meaning' hijacked through popular culture memes, in the media and even with some commercial organizations. These misconceptions suggest that a person who is organized and tidy, or someone who is pernickety and fussy, has OCD. The misuse of the acronym also insinuates that OCD is a preference or choice and fails to recognize that the D in OCD stands for disorder.

In fact, OCD impacts on every aspect of a person's life. Everyday functioning from brushing teeth, going to the toilet or going to bed can involve hours of torturous, nightmarish worries and behaviours.

The condition can have devastating consequences on a person's education at school and university, it can impact on a person's ability to pursue or maintain the career of their choice and it can also lead to difficulties in forming and maintaining all types of relationships.

A disorder may be persistent, but it's not unusual for symptoms to wax and wane over time and become a little like a roller-coaster, with the severity increasing during times of stress. But make no mistake, if somebody has OCD they will be suffering; it will be impacting on some aspect of their life, and it will be preventing them from freely living and enjoying the life they want. That's why OCD is a disorder.

➤ Is OCD a disability?

We get asked this question a lot, and whilst neither of us consider OCD a disability in our lives anymore, we both agree that the disorder has left us debilitated during the most severe times in our lived experience. OCD can become so severe for some people that they are unable to leave their homes or go to work. Therefore, in fact, Obsessive-Compulsive Disorder is considered a disability in most parts of the world.

But whether or not OCD would be considered a disability will vary from individual to individual and doesn't depend on the OCD diagnosis itself, but instead on the severity of symptoms and the impact on a person's functioning and daily living. This is what makes the question of 'is OCD a disability?' so compli-cated because it will be for one person, but not necessarily for another, and symptoms vary and fluctuate for each individual over time.

Here in the UK, the Equality Act 2010 states a person is disabled if they have a mental impairment that has a substantial and long-term (12+ months) negative effect on their ability to do normal daily activities. It does list OCD within the conditions that might be considered a disability under the act. 'Substantial' means more than minor or trivial – for example it takes much longer than it usually would to complete a daily task like getting dressed because of OCD.

The fact that OCD is considered a disability, even if we don't always consider ourselves to be disabled because of OCD, is positive, because it ensures we are afforded the law of protection from discrimination by the Equality Act 2010 and similar acts globally, such as the American Disability Act (ADA) in the USA. This ensures that those who are struggling with OCD may be eligible to ask for reasonable adjustments in the workplace or claim benefit assistance.

In order to maximize your chances of receiving additional assistance, it's important you explain and demonstrate exactly how OCD impacts on your daily functioning and what it prevents or limits you achieving, especially since OCD is often misunderstood and not recognized as a serious problem that can limit everyday activities.

➡️ Is OCD a mental illness?

Yes, OCD is considered a mental illness. However, when we talk or write about OCD, we generally tend to call it a mental health problem.

People often ask us if OCD is a mental illness, partly because they are worried about how to classify their OCD in general conversation and partly because of the stigma still surrounding mental illness. Thankfully more and more people are being open to talking about mental health problems these days, and it's not something we should be ashamed about.

The American Psychiatric Association (APA) define mental illness as 'health conditions involving changes in emotion, thinking or behaviour (or a combination of these). Mental illnesses are associated with distress and/or problems functioning in social, work or family activities.'

Traditionally, the mental health diagnostic manuals listed Obsessive-Compulsive Disorder under a group of conditions with the category of 'Anxiety Disorders', which does make sense considering the avalanche of anxiety that people with OCD experience.

Some people are reluctant to tell employers or friends that they have OCD and feel more comfortable telling them they have anxiety problems. This is technically not inaccurate, as we do consider OCD as an anxiety disorder.

We hope one day there will be such better understanding and less stigma around OCD that people will feel comfortable enough to explain they are struggling and suffering because of OCD, which shows we have more work to do to achieve that!

In summary, if we were to categorize OCD, we would consider it an anxiety disorder, which is a mental health illness or mental health problem.

➡️ What percentage of adults have OCD?

It's estimated that OCD affects between one and two per cent of the population, which to give context that will be around ten to twenty people in every thousand.

One textbook also reported that, whilst the number of people suffering with OCD might be somewhat small, a disproportionately high number of those will fall into the severe category.

➡️ What is reassurance in OCD?

Reassurance is another less obvious compulsion that many people with OCD will be engaged in without realizing it's a compulsive behaviour. The person affected by OCD will often seek reassurance in the attempt to achieve complete certainty, or to find out if what OCD is making them fear is a real threat or not.

For example, a person with obsessions that something bad might have happened to a loved one might repeatedly call or check up on them to make sure they're OK. Another example might be someone with obsessions that their loved one no longer has feelings for them repeatedly asking if their partner, friend or family member still loves them, that they haven't upset them or are going to leave them.

Reassurance doesn't only happen between loved ones; many people with OCD will at some stage seek reassurance from friends, colleagues, search engines, OCD message boards, visiting doctors, social media and many other places. Wherever OCD can be accommodated, it will certainly try its best to get what it wants. It's also important to recognize that self-reassurance is OCD in disguise, reassuring ourselves with phrases like 'It's OK, nothing bad happened', or 'It's OK, the door was definitely locked' is ultimately feeding the OCD just as much as receiving reassurance externally.

It's inevitable that when you are anxious and worried you want somebody to tell you everything is OK. It's also perfectly natural that loved ones, seeing the tortured look on our faces, try and take that anxiety away from us by offering us reassurance. Sadly, like all compulsions, this only reinforces the need to seek more reassurance the next time.

Understanding OCD

This chapter is designed to help readers get a far greater understanding about how OCD works and to recognize the mechanics and processes that drive and give OCD its power over us.

We both know from our respective journeys with OCD that in order for us to start our recovery we needed to not just know what OCD is, but also how it works. Only then could we start to untangle and make sense of our OCD.

Understanding how OCD works will be fundamental in helping us work towards recovery.

 ## How do obsessions and compulsions reinforce each other?

To fully understand OCD, it's helpful for us to understand how obsessions and compulsions reinforce each other. Different people have different experiences of the disorder because it's diverse and complex, and this question isn't about giving answers for each individual – we will leave that to the trained health professionals. However, we want to offer a general overview and this 'OCD cycle' illustration is a good place to start to help explain that process.

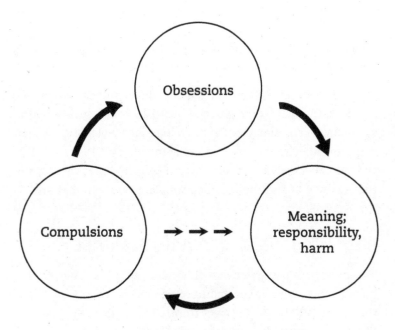

As this illustration highlights, Obsessive-Compulsive Disorder is not just about obsessions and compulsions. What happens in-between those two components is what drives this condition, which is why we both often describe the OCD as a process.

Although many people believe that the compulsions are driven by the unwanted and distressing intrusive thoughts, it's important to understand that the interpretation, or rather the misinterpretation, of those thoughts plays a big part in the cycle. The meaning that a person applies to an intrusive thought generates feelings of guilt, shame, anxiety and disgust but healthcare professionals should help you understand this with a more personalized and detailed OCD cycle illustration. We call ours the OCD roadmap but professionals may call it a vicious flower diagram. It's these emotions and the misinterpretation of them that causes a person to feel responsible and compelled to carry out a compulsion, not the thought itself.

The more the person carries out a compulsion in response to the thoughts, the more this reinforces the need to continue doing so, and a cycle of obsessions and compulsions begins. To use a well-known quote, the solution becomes the problem.

To summarize, a combination of doubt, uncertainty, misinterpretation of thoughts, a heightened sense of responsibility and a sprinkling of emotions are the main ingredients of a process that come together to create a big problem called OCD. It's not the thoughts themselves that are the problem, it's what we do with those thoughts and the meaning we place on them that are.

What is a groinal response?

When we discussed writing this book, this was one of the questions we were requested to cover. It's such a taboo subject that many OCD books shy away from, which adds to the problem that people with this symptom are less likely to seek help.

People with obsessions about being sexually attracted to someone they shouldn't, for example an authority figure, a religious leader, a child or a family member, will experience not just unwanted intrusive thoughts and worries, but frequently also experience the unwanted sensation of groinal responses whenever their OCD is triggered. It's also common for people who are experiencing obsessions with doubt about their sexual orientation to experience these unwanted responses too. The term 'groinal response' is used to identify any reaction in the genitalia, i.e. sensations, after an unwanted intrusive thought or image. Sometimes even a tingle or small movement in the genitalia will be sufficient to cause the person to believe they're aroused and reinforce a misinterpretation of their intrusive thoughts.

Of course, this movement or even arousal does not mean their obsessions prove to be factual, it simply means their body has reacted, and the more a person checks for signs of arousal, the more the body reacts. When a person is repeatedly checking for signs of arousal, this is a compulsion they feel compelled to do because they want to make sure that they aren't aroused, not because they want to be.

It's mindful attention that drives the sensation in such circumstances. For example, an exercise we both do when talking about OCD is to ask the audience to focus on one of their feet for a few seconds, and most people instantly become aware of a small tingly feeling in their foot. Now if we ask you to focus on your genitals right now, even people without OCD will notice a similar feeling or sensation. I (Ashley) explained a similar sensation when I would see dog faeces in the street; because this was one of my fears, the OCD would instantly send little tingly sensations to my nearest hand which convinced me I was contaminated.

In other words, the feeling doesn't mean anything, it just means your mind and body are talking to each other. It's also important to recognize that the reaction is because of the attention, not because of what we actually want or value.

What is an OCD avoidance?

Avoidance is a less obvious compulsion that many people with OCD will be engaged in, sometimes without even realizing it's a compulsion. An avoidance is when a person with OCD avoids the objects, places or person/people that trigger their OCD symptoms.

Let's look at an example. A person with OCD has the common obsession that they may be a paedophile, and they go to great lengths to avoid being triggered. They may go out of the room if children are visiting the family home, or they may even take themselves out of the house completely. People with this OCD theme have been known to avoid all places that children might be, i.e local parks, theme parks, shopping centres and cinemas.

The reason why people with OCD go to such great lengths to avoid their triggers is because OCD often fixates on someone's worst fears, and their obsessions bring them great distress. Some people have even gone to such extreme lengths of moving cities to avoid their potential OCD triggers.

An avoidance can be anything, and an important step to recovery is recognition of what you are avoiding and why.

What is rumination?

Ruminating is a compulsion which is generally described as going over the same thoughts and fears over and over again. There is often confusion around believing that ruminating is an obsession, but for treatment to be effective it's crucial to understand why it's not.

Although it starts with the obsession, the process of ruminating is overanalysing the intrusive thoughts repeatedly in the attempt to reduce anxiety or become completely certain about something. Ruminating involves questioning what the thoughts mean, or if the thought is in fact a real memory or completely accurate. Like the nature of all compulsions, ruminating involves a significant amount of time in distress, and it's extremely difficult to stop. Whilst we may think ruminating is helpful to solve the problem or reduce anxiety, the repeated turning over the past in our mind makes it become part of the OCD cycle process.

Are compulsions always a problem?

Yes, compulsions are always problematic in the OCD cycle process, and they have the ability to cause other compulsions to creep in here and there. The more we react to our thoughts, the more we keep the obsessions going, and the more we are re-enforcing the meaning we have placed on the thought.

However, sometimes we may need to do a compulsion to challenge a certain aspect of the OCD, and in these cases, although they are compulsions that will need challenging at some point, they can be temporary bridges to helping us get to a different destination.

For example, I (Ashley) had a fear about dog poo, and I knew the way to overcome that was to pick it up with the bag and get used to binning it, but that felt like a step too far in one go. Therefore, I went through a series of steps, and one of those steps was using gloves with the bag. However, the aim was to be able to use the bag to pick it up without any gloves next time. Whilst I was aware using the gloves was a compulsion, it was a temporary bridge to help me to work towards the long-term goal and eventually I was able to pick up the dog poo using a normal bag and without any gloves.

Another example of where a temporary compulsion might be necessary is when there's a concern over safety. For example, someone with contamination-related obsessions is washing with bleach, but this is dangerous for their health and would be much safer for them to use soap instead. Whilst compulsively washing with soap is still a compulsion, it's safer for the individual to temporarily perform the compulsion in a different and safer way, until they are ready to work towards no longer performing any compulsions with the help of a therapist.

With both of these examples, this requires self-honesty, an acknowledgment that you're doing a compulsion, and a pledge that you recognize that it's still OCD.

➤ Is limiting myself to just one or two compulsions enough?

If you're working towards no compulsions at all, and that is your clear and immediate objective, then reducing from multiple compulsions to just one or two is a fantastic achievement and is a great short-term step before attempting without compulsions.

However, if you continue to do one or two compulsions there's a risk. Checking a door is locked once or twice might not feel too risky, but it is if you're doing it in response to OCD. We have learned over the years from bitter experience that this only leads to more and more compulsions. One minute has the potential to become five minutes, five minutes can then become twenty minutes, and so on.

That's not to belittle anybody's achievements at getting hours of compulsions down to minutes. Progress is something to always be proud of, despite how much OCD may still play a part in your life. Don't let the fact that you still do a couple of compulsions take away from your hard work and persistence. However, working towards no compulsions at all is absolutely a realistic possibility.

➤ What age can someone be diagnosed with OCD?

Some people start having symptoms early in their life during childhood, but for the majority of people OCD usually starts or significantly becomes a problem during teenage years or young adulthood, in their early twenties. That said, it's not uncommon for many adults with OCD to report having symptoms in childhood, and we have certainly worked with parents who have children as young as five and six with a diagnosis of OCD.

Historically, we have worked with people who were only formally diagnosed later in adulthood, in their 40s. In all those cases the person reported having OCD for many years – sometimes decades even – prior to the formal diagnosis.

There are many factors which prevent people from reaching out for help. Fear, shame, embarrassment and a misunderstanding of the disorder in general. Sometimes people don't know they have OCD, and they are genuinely fearful they are just 'bad' people, particularly if their obsessions are that of a taboo nature. Pre-internet generations of my age (Ashley) and older often went an average of 17 years from developing symptoms until diagnosis.

Another reason people don't get diagnosed until later in life – more so in the past, but it still occasionally happens today – is because OCD was misdiagnosed to be something else, for example Generalized Anxiety Disorder (GAD).

Some people develop OCD later in life, but this is less common.

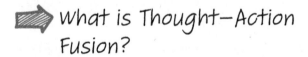 What is Thought–Action Fusion?

We've included this question because it's a clinical term that is frequently used in the context of OCD and is often misunderstood.

First off, from a language point of view, the term Thought–Action Fusion isn't the best way to explain what it means. Perhaps a better way to think of it is thought equals reality.

We have explored throughout this book how it's not the intrusive thoughts that are necessarily the driving factor in OCD, but how we interpret and respond to those thoughts. Thought-Action Fusion is common within OCD, and it is where people believe that thinking about an unwanted action or event makes it more likely that the event will happen or the equivalent to actually carrying out that action.

An example might be someone getting an image of a loved one's holiday flight crashing. They may worry that having this thought somehow increases the chances that it will happen. Another person may have a thought pop into their mind about something unacceptable, such as them deliberately harming a loved one. They may worry that having this thought is as morally bad as actually harming them. Their thinking may be something like, 'Because I had this thought it means that I am more likely to hurt my loved one, or that I must really want to hurt them'.

In summary, whilst Thought–Action Fusion is the term your therapist is most likely to use, it is simply another example of placing an over importance on thoughts.

Does OCD run in families?

This is a question we are asked all the time, along with 'what causes OCD?' and the honest answer is, we are simply not sure.

There's been plenty of research into the subject, some of which suggests there may be a strong genetic link, meaning there could be someone else in your family with OCD too. However, regardless of the amount of research, there has never been any conclusive evidence to support this theory, and other factors may also play a part. We know of people with OCD who have other family members with OCD too, but we have also spoken to individuals with OCD who have no close family member exhibit symptoms of OCD that they are aware of.

In summary, we simply know that, whilst OCD runs in some families, we don't know exactly why that is or what contributes to that occurrence.

What causes OCD?

It's common for OCD sufferers to want to know what caused them to develop this awful disorder but the truth is, we just don't know, or rather we can't say it's definitely one thing.

When discussing what causes OCD with other sufferers, you will probably notice that the room is often divided, with a mixture of different beliefs and opinions. The reason why it's a broad topic is because we all have very different lives and life experiences, and we don't believe there is one specific cause for OCD to develop. It's believed that certain factors come together to form OCD, and for each individual those factors can vary.

Some people can pinpoint the exact time they remember OCD becoming a problem, after a traumatic or life event that happened to them. Whereas some people say they remember having symptoms of OCD or anxiety before their experiences of trauma, and the event caused OCD to expand. Some people with no experiences of trauma at all say that OCD has been around for as long as they can remember, and they don't have any memory of life before OCD.

Some people with OCD have other family members who also have the disorder, which has led them to wonder if OCD is in fact genetic. However, like any other research around this topic, there's not enough conclusive evidence to prove this theory, and other factors may also play a part.

There are many other theories and opinions, but because scientists have not yet been able to identify a definite cause for why OCD can develop, there is no straightforward answer to this question. We like to stick to saying it's a combination of different factors that come together at one time, and what may have caused OCD to develop for one person, could be very different from another.

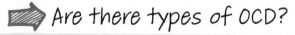

Are there types of OCD?

We don't believe there are different types of OCD, and when we talk about the disorder, we just refer to it as OCD regardless of what symptoms a person might have. However, in recent years people have started categorizing OCD into different types, and these are based off the different obsessions or compulsions a person might experience. Let's start with looking at the different types people use, based on the obsessions.

OCD can latch on to any intrusive thought, which is why different people experience different themes and obsessions, and the three most common acronyms used are SO-OCD, POCD, and ROCD.

- SO-OCD – Sexual Orientation OCD (doubting sexuality)

- POCD – Paedophile OCD (fear of being a paedophile)

- ROCD – Relationship OCD (fear of problems within a relationship)

One of the many problems with these acronyms is they have often been confused to mean different things to different people. We have also seen these acronyms to be used for a variety of other meanings including:

- HOCD = Hoarding OCD, Harm OCD

- POCD = Pure O OCD, Perinatal OCD

- ROCD = Religious OCD, Rumination OCD

There are infinite themes of obsessions, and we simply cannot categorize them all or give them acronyms of their own. Not only because there aren't enough letters in the alphabet, but also because it could lead to the hindering of the recovery progress. A person may fail to identify the problem as the OCD process and focus too much on the theme of the thoughts. This is particularly unhelpful if a person's symptoms and obsessions shift over time, which we have seen many times when working with people.

We have also seen OCD categorized into different types by behaviours, for example checking OCD, counting OCD, tapping OCD, perfectionism OCD, or just right OCD. Much like with the previous examples, it's just OCD. However, this time the different categories are based on the different types of compulsions a person might experience.

These acronyms and categories are mainly used within the online OCD community; however, they are very rarely used by health professionals. This is because they recognize the problem of categorizing a person's OCD, and the acronyms and categories are simply not accurate terms to use.

Labelling different themes and behaviours in OCD as different types can lead to complacency that OCD is not impacting on the individual in other areas of their life, because more often than not, OCD will overlap between themes/categories. For example, someone who is primarily struggling with checking behaviours may also struggle with tapping or counting behaviours. In another example, someone who is experiencing harm-related obsessions might also experience contamination-themed obsessions.

When we categorize OCD into different types, it can cause confusion over what OCD is, and it makes people believe that OCD works differently for everyone. Whilst we understand that we all experience different symptoms, emotions, obsessions, and compulsions, it's important to remember that the process and vicious cycle of OCD remains the same for everyone.

The confusion of different types can cause people to become distressed whilst searching for a particular therapist to treat their 'type' of OCD, and it can also make people fear they are 'abnormal' or have a 'worse' type.

To sum up, the different types that people talk about are simply referring to the different types of obsessions or compulsions. Regardless of what type of intrusive thoughts you get, what symptoms you struggle with, or what compulsions you carry out, it's just OCD. It will involve both obsessions and compulsions, and treatment approaches would be no different. Therefore, the only three acronyms we like to refer to are OCD, and the therapeutic treatments that lead to recovery: CBT with ERP!

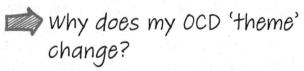 Why does my OCD 'theme' change?

One of the reasons why OCD can cause so much distress is because it often attacks what is most important and valuable to us. For example, a religious person with OCD might struggle with blasphemous thoughts, whereas a new parent might suffer from distressing obsessions related to their child. When life changes and new challenges arise, OCD has the tendency to jump to something else and fixate on what is important in a person's life at that time.

It's important to note that some people who are suffering because of OCD find that the theme isn't necessarily linked to a person's values or holds a significant amount of importance. Sometimes it's just a case of OCD knowing what bothers us, with no logical explanation. Remember, the themes are just based on thoughts, and because thoughts and fears naturally change throughout life, OCD can too.

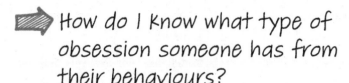 ## How do I know what type of obsession someone has from their behaviours?

You can't guess what type of obsession someone has based on their behaviours. For example, you could see two people with OCD washing and furiously scrubbing their hands. You might assume that both of them are doing so because they are afraid of germs, however, OCD goes far deeper than that.

The first person has a worry that their loved ones will become ill if they haven't scrubbed perceived contamination from their hands. They worry that their loved one will die, the family will become hurt, and it'll be all their fault. Whereas the second person has an obsession that they are a disgusting person, and they furiously scrub because they don't want to feel disgusting. As you can see, in both of these examples the behaviours are exactly the same, however the obsessions behind those behaviours are completely different.

How do I know if I am doing something because I enjoy it or because OCD is making me?

This question has come up a few times over the years and is a good question because it can help you understand if you still have work to do on challenging your OCD. The rule of thumb is if you feel you can carry on with your day without completing the activity, then it probably wasn't a compulsion.

It's something we have spoken about at OCD support groups over the years, and I (Ashley) tell the story from my own journey of how after almost two decades having a bath daily because OCD forced me to carry out strict washing behaviours, I now have a relaxing soak in a hot bubble bath because I want to, not because I feel compelled to by the demands of OCD.

However, be mindful of OCD in disguise. For example, let's say you used to have to keep your toothbrush in your bedroom because the bathroom was contaminated, but in recovery you still keep the toothbrush in your bedroom out of preference. Be honest with yourself if it really is a preference, or if OCD is still lurking underneath the floorboards. If in doubt, behave anti-OCD and keep the toothbrush in the bathroom anyway.

⟹ Why can't people with OCD just stop the compulsions?

Let's look at what happens in-between an obsession and a compulsion. When someone with OCD has an intrusive thought, they attempt to apply meaning to it, despite the thought being completely meaningless. Applying meaning to the thought generates feelings of guilt, shame, anxiety, a heightened sense of responsibility, disgust and many other negative feelings. These feelings make it extremely difficult to resist carrying out a compulsion and break the vicious cycle of OCD.

Although the meaning applied to the thought is a misconception, to the person suffering it isn't a misconception at all – the threat feels very much real. Imagine a scenario where someone extremely important to you is about to walk out in to moving traffic, your natural instinct would be to stop it and react to this threat. Because people with OCD feel like their obsessions are real threats, they respond as if they are.

Debunking OCD Myths

Most people who stigmatize OCD do so with no ill intensions or malice, but the long-term effects of misuse of the term are damaging. When people say phrases like 'I am a little bit OCD', it trivializes a serious problem and makes it appear to be a personality trait we all have to some extent. Phrases like this might sound harmless, but they add to the stigma behind the condition, which reinforces feelings of shame for people who are suffering. Those feelings of shame can prevent people from reaching out for help, which sadly leads to a delayed diagnosis and recovery. Any second spent battling OCD is a second too long, and nobody should have to do it alone.

Although there is increased awareness about OCD, there is still a lot of misinformation out there. Because of this, we are always committed to spending our time debunking the myths behind the condition.

We feel this chapter is important, not just for those wanting to learn new ways to challenge misuse as service users, but for those who want to learn more about the reality of OCD compared to the incorrect assumptions of the condition that society has created.

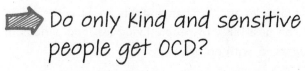

Do only kind and sensitive people get OCD?

It's often believed that only people who are sensitive, kind and overly caring can develop Obsessive-Compulsive Disorder.

This isn't completely true because the condition can affect anyone regardless of their character.

However, if we were to generalize, then we would say that OCD usually happens to people who are too nice for their own good. Loving parents develop OCD around harming children, gentle people develop OCD around being violent and people who are religious develop OCD around their faith.

Being a sensitive and conscientious person can be one of the factors that makes some people more vulnerable to developing OCD, which is possibly why this is such a commonly asked question.

Does everybody have a little bit of OCD?

It's often falsely believed that everybody 'is a little bit OCD', but it's important to remember that OCD is not an adjective. Obsessive-Compulsive Disorder is exactly what it says in the name – a disorder. You can't have a little bit of a disorder, you either have one or you don't.

We can understand why people might *think* it's a personality trait we all have a bit of, because misuse of the term is sadly widespread across society. That being said, although it's important to understand why someone might think this, it's more important to challenge misuse of the term when it occurs. Knowledge is power and the truths about OCD need revealing to the world. It's not a joke – it's extremely debilitating. We have a collective responsibility to change the way people talk about this horrific disorder and, by changing this, we have the ability to prevent the possibility of people living for long periods of time undiagnosed, with no help.

People like order, routine and checking things are done correctly. It makes us human. But there is a big difference between checking the straighteners are off before you leave the house and spending long periods of time checking in a state of anxiety, distress and pure exhaustion. There is a huge difference between feeling uncomfortable after having an intrusive thought, and completely attacking your character, punishing yourself and taking the most extreme measures to prevent that thought from becoming reality.

For many people with OCD, the 'everyone has a bit of OCD' misconception is the most frustrating one. When OCD has stripped you of all your energy, dampened your spark and convinced you that you are a disgusting and terrible human being, hearing the disorder being trivialized is extremely deflating. It diminishes the gruelling experiences you have endured and replaces it with something so average.

To conclude the answer to this question: no, we don't all have a bit of OCD. We all like things to look nice, neat and tidy. We all like making sure that people are safe, and our loved ones are well. We all like having a routine and sticking to it daily. We all have intrusive thoughts that make us feel uncomfortable or shocked. But we don't all have Obsessive-Compulsive Disorder. The point where it becomes a disorder is when it's taking over our lives, causing distress and severely impacting our everyday lives. The misconceptions mean that when we try to explain our condition to other people, they don't understand how serious and devastating it really is to live with.

Do people with OCD all have spotless homes?

There are two problems with this question. The first is that this creates the idea that everyone with OCD is supposed to experience the same symptoms, obsessions, feelings and compulsions. The second is that this reinforces the misunderstanding that people with OCD like cleaning their houses.

Not everybody with OCD experiences compulsions that involve repeatedly cleaning their homes, however for those who do, this means they are in a state of distress as they do so. People with OCD don't enjoy doing their compulsions and they don't find them satisfying or therapeutic. They are carrying out these behaviours in response to distressing intrusive thoughts.

In fact, in some cases, cleaning compulsions can be so severe they can lead to a person completely avoiding household chores, which inevitably builds up to cause poor cleanliness, hygiene and organization. For example, if a sufferer is aware that cleaning their home means coming into contact with contaminated objects or places, they might be unable to tolerate such distress which could result in the avoidance of cleaning completely. In another example, for a sufferer to clean their home they might need to perform compulsions a particular number of times, or until it feels just right, and so avoiding the chores is a less mentally exhausting option for them.

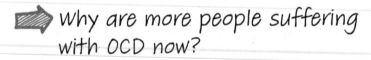 Why are more people suffering with OCD now?

We are frequently asked if more people suffer with OCD now than in the past, but we don't think that's the case. There's a possibility that more people are being diagnosed than previously simply due to increased research and awareness. However, this doesn't necessarily mean more people are suffering from OCD, it just means fewer people are suffering silently without a diagnosis.

The media also have a part to play in the misconception that more people are suffering with OCD. They make lots of references to the disorder, often inaccurately, to project a preference for liking things a certain way which makes it appear that more people have it.

In summary, we don't think OCD is more common today than it used to be, it's just talked about more, which can be helpful for those who actually have it, but counter-productive if a large part of the awareness is stigma-based information.

Will an ex-sufferer be the best therapist to help me because they have experienced OCD?

Not necessarily, no. We have both looked for private therapists in the past and neither of us set out to specifically find an ex-sufferer turned therapist, we just looked to find the best therapist to help us.

In recent years social media has become flooded with ex-sufferers who offer various chargeable treatment approaches (under guises ranging from coach to therapist), however, we recommend to always check out an individual's professional medical qualifications.

Is hoarding part of OCD?

Traditionally, people who experienced hoarding problems were long considered to be suffering from Obsessive-Compulsive Disorder, but in 2013 hoarding problems were reclassified to be a disorder in their own right. This is where it gets complicated, because those who hoard items could still be considered to have OCD. We will try and explain how the two might be confused.

If a person has problems discarding and parting with possessions, and it causes significant distress to do so, it can be classified as hoarding disorder. This can often lead to disorganization and clutter in the home, making it difficult to live in. Also, a strong urge to acquire items is commonplace with hoarding disorder.

However, it's somewhat complicated by the fact that some people with OCD also hoard. Perhaps one key difference is that with OCD there will be very specific obsessive worries, feelings and fears (such as something bad will happen if the person discards certain objects or items), that most would consider discardable. In OCD, the items are usually less likely to result in clutter to the point of being unable to use the room. In this scenario the mental health diagnostic manual suggests it would be better explained as OCD.

In recent years hoarding has received significant and sensationalized TV coverage, in part because of the seemingly shocking conditions that those with hoarding disorder live in. People suffering with hoarding or clutter problems are often referred to as a 'hoarder', however it's important to remember a person can't be a problem, just like we would not call somebody with OCD an OCDer.

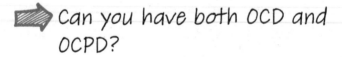 ## Can you have both OCD and OCPD?

Obsessive-Compulsive Personality Disorder (OCPD) and Obsessive-Compulsive Disorder (OCD) sound the same, but not withstanding similar names, they are in fact two separate conditions, but their similarities make it difficult to distinguish between the two. Somebody could be diagnosed with either condition but could also be diagnosed with both simultaneously.

Whilst OCD is considered an anxiety disorder, OCPD, as the name suggests, is actually a personality disorder. The main features of OCPD is a preoccupation with orderliness, perfectionism at the expense of flexibility, openness and efficiency, regardless of the impact on others.

Despite the similarity in names, OCD is usually easily distinguished from OCPD by the presence of the unwanted intrusive thoughts and worries – true obsessions. People with OCD often feel distressed by the nature of their behaviours or thoughts, even if they are unable to control them. People with OCPD, however, typically believe that their actions have a practical aim and purpose.

➡️ Shouldn't people with OCD just laugh off OCD jokes?

This question can be more easily answered when put into the perspective of another condition. For example, can you imagine witnessing someone asking a person with cancer why they can't just laugh off jokes about cancer? Absolutely not. That would be highly inappropriate, insensitive and morally unacceptable. People with OCD should be offered the same level of respect that any other person with any other condition or illness should be offered.

One of the problems with jokes about OCD is that they are often designed in a way that makes OCD look easy to deal with and quirky. Nobody should expect people with OCD to laugh off jokes that make their challenging experiences look like a walk in the park. Sadly, being expected to laugh at these types of jokes shows us just how much work we still have to do when it comes to education surrounding OCD.

We are aware that most people make such jokes due to the lack of understanding about the condition, rather than out of malice or intent to offend anyone.

➡️ Why do people with OCD get upset when OCD is trivialized?

There are many different reasons why trivialization can be so upsetting for people with OCD, and one of the main ones is that it can leave people feeling invalidated and misunderstood. This can then cause them to bottle up their feelings and refrain from reaching out to others, when what they really need is to be listened to, supported and guided in the right direction for help. It's often the long-term effects of trivialization that are so problematic and devastating.

People with OCD aren't the only ones who find trivialization upsetting. Parents, caregivers, partners, family members and friends of people with OCD can find it upsetting too. It's hard for loved ones of people with OCD to see the disorder being trivialized so casually, when they know the pure anguish that their loved one has endured, and how much it has affected their own lives and mental health too.

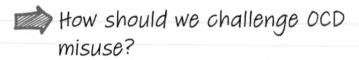 How should we challenge OCD misuse?

It can be so difficult to remain calm and collected when someone is trivializing a disorder which has caused a significant amount of distress in our lives, and it's completely normal to feel angry and hurt as a natural response to trivialization. However, there are constructive ways in which we can respond to such comments which have the power to possibly change the way someone envisions and talks about Obsessive-Compulsive Disorder.

We have found that the best way to challenge misuse is to start by understanding why someone is misinformed about the realities of OCD, and to make it clear to that person that we understand why they are misinformed.

It's society's responsibility as a collective to change the way people talk about OCD, but it's not one person's fault that stigma exists. Once we have explained to this person, or organization, that we understand why they are misinformed, we can then move on to explaining why what they have said is so problematic. Sometimes it isn't about what we say, it is the way we say it. In our experience, addressing the situation in an empathetic, non-judgemental way will receive a much more positive response, and it may even open up the conversation to talk further about how serious OCD really is.

People make mistakes, and when certain phrases have been part of society's vocabulary for so long, it's only natural that slip-of-the-tongue references are made here and there. It doesn't mean that those people are bad people or that they have intentions to deliberately cause offence. The problem with responding to those natural feelings of anger and frustration is that this could change what could be an opportunity for an educational and informative conversation into an argumentative debate where people become defensive.

Secondly, try to figure out if the person who has made the comment has done this to provoke a reaction. Regardless of how sensitively you approach the subject, there are going to be people who think that this 'snowflake' generation are making a mountain out of a molehill, and that OCD isn't a serious problem. There will be people who want to argue this with you, and won't listen to understand, but listen to respond. Rise above thoughtless negative comments and don't waste your energy engaging in these types of conversations.

Thirdly, consider whether now is the right time. Conversations at a time of high stress and anxiety may lead to frustrations that impact the clarity of our message. This is also relevant in other social settings, such as moments of joy and celebrations. Could bringing up a serious conversation during a joyous moment in the company of many different individuals cause embarrassment, tension and irritability? Absolutely. It's OK if we need to hold off and address the problem at a more socially acceptable and convenient time.

But above all, remember that challenging OCD misuse can become tiresome. For our own sake, creating a gentle and non-judgemental conversation will protect our own energy as much as anything else. It's important to remember that if we don't feel like using our own experiences with OCD as an opportunity to educate, we can still challenge misuse in other ways. We could explain that recently we have learned a lot about OCD, and we thought it would be useful to share these learnings with others.

Remember, it isn't personal. It is just going to take some time to unravel years' worth of trivialization, and we can do it together. One step at a time.

Remember that if you don't feel emotionally strong enough to challenge OCD stigma – that is OK too. OCD is an incredibly exhausting condition to battle, and it's important to protect your own energy and mental wellbeing when you need to.

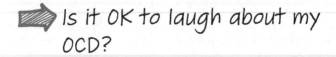 Is it OK to laugh about my OCD?

Some people with OCD use laughter as a coping mechanism. It's completely natural to find humour as you look back over the embarrassing situations that OCD has led you to, despite how distressed and mentally unwell you were at the time. We do, however, encourage people to be mindful of humour surrounding someone else's experiences with OCD.

Finding humour in dark places isn't everyone's preference, and some people might not be far enough along in the recovery journey to be able to find anything funny at all. It's important to let people set the tone regarding humour surrounding their own lived experiences with OCD. After all, there is absolutely nothing funny about living with OCD.

Children and OCD

Sufferers themselves aren't the only people who struggle to know how to cope or respond to the demands of this disorder. For parents and caregivers, supporting a child with OCD is an extremely challenging and distressing process. Sadly, they are often left feeling unheard, unsupported and isolated.

In this chapter, we aim to restore hope for parents and caregivers by exploring some of the most frequently asked questions, addressing common myths and challenging misinformation that surrounds this topic.

Is it my fault my child has OCD?

It can be easy to blame yourself if your child is suffering because of Obsessive-Compulsive Disorder, but you can't give someone a mental health problem, and you aren't a bad parent because your child is struggling.

Some people with OCD can pinpoint the specific time or place that they remember OCD becoming a problem, whereas others have spent years wondering how or why they developed it. It's believed that OCD develops due to a combination of different factors that come together at one time, and because people all have very different lives, those factors can vary from person to person.

There are many different theories on what might cause OCD, but little evidence for many of them. However, we do not believe that OCD reflects the way someone has been parented, and even the most knowledgeable professionals put OCD down to just pure bad luck. We might never know why your child has developed OCD, but we do know how to treat it, and that is the most important thing.

➡ Does giving my child reassurance make OCD worse?

When someone with OCD is repeatedly asking for reassurance, this is a compulsion. Reassurance-seeking is often not recognized as a compulsion because it isn't as obvious as other physical compulsions. However, because the reassurance is a behaviour being carried out with an intent to neutralize anxiety or in response to a heightened sense of responsibility, the reassurance is buying into the fears and reinforcing the OCD.

However, this puts parents and caregivers in an impossible position, because whilst you may be aware that giving reassurance is feeding the OCD, you also have a natural instinct to reassure your child, make them feel safe, and relieve them from anxiety and distress. We don't think it's talked about enough just how difficult this is for parents and caregivers, and we are continuously inspired by those who support loved ones with OCD every day.

It's important for your own mental wellbeing, and your relationship with your child, not to take on the role of a therapist. Your job is to parent your child, emotionally support them and help them to feel empowered to overcome this. It would be unfair for anyone to expect you, as your child's parent, to fix this problem and treat the OCD yourself.

If you were to suddenly stop giving your child reassurance, this could become quite counterproductive and cause even more distress for everyone involved, particularly if there has been a lot of reassurance-seeking at home. Although the end goal is to stop the reassurance, there are some challenges that your child just won't be ready to tackle yet without the help of a therapist, and reassurance-seeking might be one of those challenges.

That being said, some families have found some subtle ways to try and reduce reassurance-seeking, particularly when things are getting out of hand and the waiting list for treatment is lengthy. For example, if their child has already asked for reassurance many times, they have experimented with responding with phrases like 'Is this OCD asking, because if so, OCD is a bully, and I can't answer this question again because I am on your side.' Remember, you aren't expected to try this, and you may wish to wait for therapeutic intervention before planning a way to reduce reassurance seeking at home. Don't forget, you're not your child's therapist, and you matter too.

➡ Will my child's future be severely impacted by OCD?

One of the most dangerous myths to stumble across is that everybody with OCD will always live a life heavily impacted by the disorder. This myth is misleading, and as a parent it's probably the most terrifying myth to read. However, the truth is people in recovery and those still on their recovery journey from OCD can have relationships, a successful career, a social life and, more importantly, be just as happy as someone without lived experience of OCD.

Just because OCD can have the ability to impact someone's future, it doesn't mean everyone will experience this. For some people with OCD, a late diagnosis or a long time spent without the right help or guidance has sadly caused OCD to take over a large period of their lives. Recognizing OCD is the problem early on or during childhood can reduce the chances of a life heavily impacted by OCD, but that doesn't mean recognizing

OCD at a later age means they can't recover and take back their life.

➡️ How do I know if the therapy my child is receiving is good therapy?

This is a very common worry that parents and caregivers experience when their child is in treatment for OCD, particularly if there has been a long wait to receive the therapy.

Recovery from OCD isn't something you can achieve overnight – it takes time. It's crucial that we give therapy a chance to work because progress is a gradual process, noticeable changes don't often happen straight away and we also appreciate that everyone progresses at their own pace. However, we do recommend that if there haven't been any positive changes at all, however small, within around a dozen sessions, then it might be a good idea to evaluate whether something needs to change. Whether that be the introduction of medication, a different therapy approach or a change of therapist if possible.

This doesn't mean that if after a dozen sessions your child hasn't progressed, their therapist isn't a competent one (although, it can mean that of course) – it isn't always as black and white as that. Sometimes it boils down to something as simple as the chemistry not being quite right, or this particular therapist's approach not suiting your child. A therapist that has proven to be helpful for one child might not be for another. Remember, everyone is different, and we all respond to people and characters differently. This is why it's so important to stay focused on your own journey, and not compare it to anyone else's.

In some cases, if no progression has been made, it could be as simple as the therapist not being knowledgeable enough in understanding Obsessive-Compulsive Disorder, and a therapist who has a better understanding of how it works is needed. Regardless of the reason why it isn't working, your child deserves to experience therapy that is effective and that helps them to overcome OCD.

In our experience, there are certain qualities in a therapist which could indicate that your child is receiving good therapy. A good therapist should engage with your child and discuss the therapeutic techniques. Understanding the techniques is important, as this will help your child to engage in therapy, because they understand what the short-term and long-term goals are.

Secondly, a good therapist will help your child to choose to change. If your child is only engaging in certain tasks because they have been told to, or they don't want to disappoint anyone by not engaging, this could mean your child doesn't understand the importance of recovery and how the aim is to be better for their own sake, and not anybody else's.

And thirdly, a good therapist won't be afraid to get their hands dirty too, sometimes in a literal sense. For example, we have known a therapist to get completely involved with exposure tasks with their patient, including exercises like putting their hands down a toilet bowl and rubbing the water through their hair! This is known as an exposure exercise, which we explain more about in Chapter 7. If your child's therapist is involving themselves in the experiments and the exercises, this is a good sign. Therapy for OCD should be a collaborative approach between therapist and patient.

➡ Is my child too young for treatment?

There is nothing in the national treatment guidelines for OCD that talks about a minimum age for Cognitive Behavioural

Therapy (the recommended treatment for OCD). That being said, it's important for a therapist to deliver the therapy at an age-appropriate level of a child's understanding. For younger children, where understanding isn't there, therapy might take longer, and it might take longer to explain certain aspects of therapy.

Should we tell the school?

This decision is a personal choice, and deciding about whether to inform a school will depend on you and your child's preferences. For younger children, there is often very little attempt to hide their symptoms, which could mean teaching staff may already be aware of certain behaviours. Older children and adolescents, however, may be able to hide their symptoms from their friends and teachers more easily. Regardless of age and circumstances, your child may be under tremendous stress due to the impact of OCD on schoolwork, and informing the school could be a beneficial and supportive move.

Consistency is key when it comes down to fighting OCD, and if your child is receiving therapeutic help, which involves certain approaches and therapeutic techniques at home, it would be extremely beneficial for your child's teachers to be on the same page to avoid any unravelling of progress.

That being said, we know that some children and young people are reluctant to tell the school about their experiences with OCD for many reasons, such as shame, guilt, embarrassment or fear of judgement. At this point, you might feel as though you are stuck between a rock and a hard place. You don't want to tell the school without your child's permission, but equally you know that the school knowing will help them in their recovery. In these circumstances, we would recommend talking through the positives that telling the school would bring and try to guide your child in to making their own decision of telling the school about OCD.

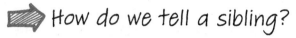# How do we tell a sibling?

It can be difficult to know what to say to a sibling about your other child's experiences with OCD, and the best way to approach this can vary depending on individual circumstances. Some parents/caregivers with very young children might decide not to talk to them about the OCD at this stage, which of course is totally understandable and a very personal choice. However, in some circumstances where siblings are very much involved in the OCD's compulsions and demands, informing them might be the most appropriate decision.

In other cases, the OCD can cause siblings to develop a difficult relationship. This can not only be upsetting for your children to experience, but it can also be difficult for you to witness, particularly if before the OCD they had a close relationship. This is another example of why you might want to inform the sibling about the OCD; this way they can understand why their relationship has become strained instead of blaming their sibling for the changed behaviour.

This brings us on to the original question: how do we tell their sibling?

Well, this is very much a personal choice also, and there are some different routes you can take with this. If the sibling is a younger child, you could use the 'brain bully' analogy. It's an analogy that has proven to be quite helpful for children to understand how OCD works. For example, if a bully in the playground at school tells your child they have to give them their dinner money or else they will beat them up, what would you tell your child? You would tell them if they gave the bully the money they would come back for more. This is exactly how OCD works too. The more we give OCD the compulsions it asks for, the more powerful it becomes.

OCD sees our weaknesses just like real-life bullies do, and it plays on those weaknesses to gain power. Whilst a child might find it hard to understand an invisible condition, they generally understand how bullies work and why it's important to challenge a bully's behaviour. By using this analogy, the sibling might be able to understand why as a family you are finding things hard and trying to stick to a plan when challenging OCD's bullying behaviours.

If the sibling isn't a child, and is more into their teenage years, the bully analogy might feel quite patronising. In this case, you might want to use particular literature created for teens with OCD. There are lots of different flyers, podcasts, vlogs etc that can help with this. These resources have a great way of explaining what OCD is in a bite-sized and simplistic way.

However, regardless of our advice, you are the experts when it comes to understanding your children's needs, how they process information and understand problems and difficulties. The majority of the time this will all be by preference and your own evaluation of the situation. Remember, it's OK if the way you talk about OCD to your children is different from another parents' method.

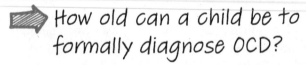 How old can a child be to formally diagnose OCD?

The answer to this question is quite fluid. This is because a diagnosis for young children can be quite complicated. We have worked with parents who have children as young as five and six with a diagnosis of Obsessive-Compulsive Disorder. However, we recognize a diagnosis for a young child can come with some barriers.

Some childlike behaviours can look like OCD, so it can often be hard to differentiate between the disorder and average childhood behaviours when assessing if the problem is OCD. It all depends on how much of an impact the symptoms are having on your child's everyday activities.

Although we have never worked with any parents who have a child under the age of five with a diagnosis of OCD, research shows that children even younger than this have been diagnosed with the disorder.

➡️ Can my child with OCD get help from school?

Your child should be entitled to additional help and support at school. Living with OCD is extremely hard, and the pressure to study whilst suffering from this disorder can be extremely overwhelming.

SENCO stands for Special Educational Needs Co-ordinator, and every school in the UK is obliged to have one within their team. A SENCO's responsibility is to co-ordinate any relevant additional support for pupils with special education needs and liaise with their caregivers and teachers.

If your child's OCD symptoms are affecting their schoolwork, ability to participate in lessons and overall productivity, you can organize a chat with the school to talk through the best way your child can be supported through their education.

Getting additional help from school can be really helpful as it adds to your child's support network. The more we all start to close in on OCD, the harder it is for the disorder to seep through the gaps. Support networks come in all shapes and sizes, and a team can be two people or ten people. Regardless, it's a team, and it's bigger and better than OCD.

My child won't talk to me about OCD, what can I do?

Firstly, we would like to start by saying it isn't your fault. OCD is a very complex disorder and it's normal for a child to struggle to talk about it to their parents, or to anyone at all.

Our advice would be to try to explore the reasons why they are struggling to open up about OCD if that's at all possible. You could ask, 'I know you don't want to talk to me about it, and that's OK, you don't have to. But could you explain why you are struggling to?' Once you know what the barriers are, it can be easier to find possible solutions to them. If they are struggling to answer this question, you could write down some of the most common reasons that children struggle to talk and ask them to circle the ones that apply to them.

One reason might be because they are too embarrassed, ashamed or disgusted to be able to talk to you about some of the problems they are experiencing. OCD thrives off these emotions, and telling others about their symptoms might further enhance these feelings.

Another reason might be because the nature of the obsessions are based around you; this is common because OCD tends to attach itself to the people or things that are most important to a person. For example, they may be experiencing obsessions that harm might come to you, or that you are contaminated or will become contaminated because of them. In these circumstances, it's common for the child to avoid talking about OCD to just one parent, which can leave that specific parent feeling like it's personal, which of course it isn't.

Another reason might be because they just can't explain how they feel, or barely understand it themselves, so explaining it to someone else is too difficult or scary. Not talking about it could even be part of the OCD itself, for example, they could have obsessions that if they say their fears out loud, it could come true.

It's also common for children and young people to become confused with 'just right' obsessions. This is where they perform compulsions because they have a feeling they need to, to prevent something bad from happening, and to relieve that feeling and anxiety. They might struggle to explain this to you because they don't actually know why they feel the way they do or need to do the compulsions.

Regardless of the many different reasons why a child isn't opening up about their problems with OCD, it isn't anybody's fault, it's very normal, and it can sometimes take time.

One option you could look into exploring is using a tick box booklet. It might be that your child is struggling to come to terms with the types of intrusive thoughts they are having, therefore using a booklet where they can tick boxes that explain the extent of their problems is easier than saying it out loud or writing it down. You can find booklets like these on OCD charity websites.

Another option could be to encourage them to watch videos and read blogs created by other young people with OCD, as this could normalize their experiences with the disorder if they hear others with very similar obsessions, compulsions and feelings. Witnessing others talk openly about their experiences might help them to understand their own.

You might have already exhausted all these suggestions and have had no luck with any progress. In these circumstances, sometimes the confidence to talk openly about OCD comes with time and therapeutic intervention. As they start to understand their own thought patterns and feelings with the help of a therapist, it could increase their confidence to talk to you about the OCD.

Remember, big changes often start with small steps, and it might take some time for your child to be in a position to open up. This doesn't mean you aren't doing a good job at supporting your child, and it doesn't mean you have done anything wrong. If they know that when they are ready to talk, you will be there to listen, they will feel supported, and you are doing enough.

Don't forget, it isn't your responsibility to fix this. You are not your child's therapist, and your own mental wellbeing matters just as much. If you have found out the reason why your child is struggling to open up about the OCD, but you aren't quite sure how to challenge the problem, that's OK. Reach out to a professional for some advice on how to overcome this hurdle, and if that isn't possible right now, make a note for when that time comes.

How do I respond to my child's anger and frustration?

Anger and frustration are very normal emotions to feel when battling OCD and it's very hard for parents to know how to respond to such emotions. It's helpful to begin with understanding why these emotions can occur.

Anger can sometimes be an emotion that's driven by fear, and it's normal to react in a frustrated or angry way when you are fearful or anxious about something. For example, if a car pulls out on you on a busy roundabout and it causes you to have to make an emergency stop, your initial feeling would be fear that you would crash, or something bad was about to happen. However, very often what is manifested is what is commonly referred to as 'road rage'.

The fear and anxiety that OCD causes can sometimes manifest as anger. Whilst it's completely understandable that your child experiences these emotions, it's important to be clear that this reaction to the emotions is not acceptable. It's OK to feel angry, but it isn't OK to take it out on others.

Much like with anxiety, anger will always peak, and then come back down again. Therefore, it's better to address their behaviour when they are calm and collected, and not during the peak of their anger or frustration.

Making a clear plan with boundaries can be a helpful strategy. For example, if when they are angry, they kick and shout at others, could an alternative be to scream into a pillow or kick a football? Create these constructive alternatives during a calm time when they are not likely to react with more anger and frustration.

Remember that you matter too. If their anger is causing harm or upset to you, you have every right to remove yourself from the room and situation until you feel it's right or safe for you to do so.

Lifestyle

For those of us who live with OCD, we know only too well that the tentacles of this condition can reach every aspect of our lives. OCD can affect relationships, working, dating, paying bills and even driving to the shops. The collateral damage that OCD can cause can make every day activities extremely challenging.

In this chapter, we attempt to answer some questions which will help empower you to better cope with some of these challenges.

 ## Will my period make OCD worse?

The fact that this question is asked so frequently is no surprise to us at all. Although there is no definite or clear evidence to prove this is scientifically possible, there are many people who have reported that their OCD symptoms worsen during menstruation.

We are not doctors, but we do know that hormones can make people feel more vulnerable, and they can make challenges that people are used to facing every day feel bigger, more aggressive and more exhausting. It makes sense that some people struggle to fight OCD during their period more than they do on the average day.

If you are someone who finds that OCD feels worse during a period, or during the most hormonal stages in your cycle, remember that you aren't alone. It's completely normal.

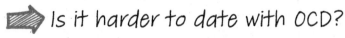 # Is it harder to date with OCD?

Sometimes, yes. The challenges people with OCD might face when dating vary depending on how someone experiences OCD. For example, someone who is experiencing contamination obsessions related to sexual bodily fluids might find intimacy too challenging. This might result in the avoidance of dating or discontinuing the dates once they start to develop into sexual relationships.

When OCD is trying to convince you that you are a bad person, disgusting, careless or irresponsible, it's hard not to experience feelings of low self-esteem and poor self-confidence. These feelings can cause problems when dating, or cause people to avoid dating altogether.

It's also common for people with OCD to have such low self-esteem that they feel they don't deserve to be happy, to have someone care for them or to love and be loved in return. This can be difficult for not only the people with OCD, but for the people who have relations with them. For some people, the biggest barrier they face is the fear of judgement or how someone might react once they have told them they have OCD.

These examples are by no means the limit of the different complications that OCD can cause when dating, and whatever the reason for which you find dating with OCD difficult, remember you aren't alone. This is just what OCD does best – it likes to take control over the things and people we care about.

OCD can cause problems for people in existing relationships and marriages, too. For example, if someone develops OCD when they are in a relationship, or if they have a setback, this can put strain on relationships and cause similar complications and difficulties.

It's also important to note that not everyone who is suffering because of Obsessive-Compulsive Disorder will find dating or relationships any more difficult than someone without OCD. OCD can affect people very differently, and that's OK.

When should I tell a new partner about my OCD?

In truth, there is no right or wrong time to tell your new partner that you suffer with OCD – that moment will eventually feel right.

From our experiences talking to people, we have learned that people have different approaches to this. Some people have found telling their partner straight away was better, because their reaction helped them to find out if they were the right person for them. Whereas others found that drip-feeding it slowly over time was helpful, starting with telling them it's OCD and gradually saying more over time. The more you get to know and trust them, the more comfortable you feel opening up about the little details and hard parts to talk about.

One thing we will say is that if not telling them is causing problems in the relationship, it's probably a good idea to say at least something about it. We both hope when you do tell your partner that you are met with kindness, love and compassion, which will only strengthen your relationship. If your partner responds negatively, then maybe they just need a little time to understand, so be patient. However, if your partner is not supportive – whilst we know it's easy for us to say this – perhaps it's better you know now.

Choosing that 'perfect moment' really does need to be your decision, but ultimately only share what you feel comfortable sharing, when you feel ready to share.

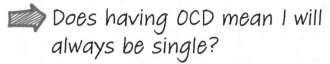 ## Does having OCD mean I will always be single?

There's no denying that suffering from Obsessive-Compulsive Disorder can make engaging in social events, dating and relationships harder and potentially even impossible at times, but there's also no reason why we can't find love.

When we live with OCD, we often find it hard to get out and socialize, and so we may need to be prepared to work to put ourselves in positions to meet potential new partners. Some examples of what you can do to maximize your success includes joining dating websites and asking friends out to social events, even if it's just for a coffee or lunch. If there are social events at work, go along to them. Even if you don't meet the one, it will ensure you enjoy yourself instead of spending an evening in with OCD, and it will allow you to break out of your comfort zone.

 ## Should I look for a partner who also has OCD?

We don't believe there is any reason to specifically look for a partner who also has OCD. We understand why people might think having a partner with OCD will help, because they understand how OCD makes us feel, they might be patient when compulsions are needed and they may be enthusiastic in helping to challenge the OCD. However, we also know from our own first-hand experiences that this can also come from a loving partner who doesn't have OCD.

We have both lived with OCD whilst being single, but neither of us have specifically looked for nor avoided love from within the OCD community. We can't choose who we fall in love with, and whether that person happens to suffer with Obsessive-Compulsive Disorder or not, let that love flourish.

Does exercise help with OCD?

There's much literature that exerts the benefits of exercise to improve our mental wellbeing, but there is no evidence that exercise specifically removes OCD. However, many of the people we work with talk positively about how exercise really helps them cope better both with general everyday stresses and anxieties, and sometimes with their OCD.

Exercise doesn't just mean running or cycling; it can be anything that gets us moving more – even gardening or walking can achieve this. Anything that leads to our body and brain being looked after has the ability to improve our mood, and when we look after our general mental wellbeing, this can have a positive follow-on effect on how we cope with OCD.

Can people with OCD claim benefits?

Yes, some people with OCD might be eligible to claim benefits, either because the condition affects their financial income, or because it prevents them from being able to work.

We know sometimes people are reluctant to ask for help, often because of the stigma attached to benefits because of how some aspects of the media discuss claiming help, but there's no shame in asking for, and receiving, additional support. Benefits are part of the society we have created, and they support us on those occasions where we're struggling to manage.

For some benefits, you'll need to have an assessment to make sure you meet the criteria to receive that benefit, which can be daunting in itself, but don't let this put you off claiming. Please don't worry if you are refused – through our work we know that many people with OCD have been successful when appealing decisions. Local or national charities will be able to offer some advice to help you understand what benefits you can claim and where to start.

⟹ Can I get help with water bills?

Does OCD mean you use a significant amount of water? If so, then you might be eligible for a scheme called WaterSure in some parts of the UK, which means your annual water bill is capped.

The capped amount means that because of having OCD, you do not have to pay any more than the average metered bill for the area. The cap amount does vary between water companies and geographical areas so you would need to check with your water company what the rate is.

Not everybody will be eligible for WaterSure and in some cases, especially if you live alone, your normal metered water bill could be less than your water company's WaterSure cap.

If you're not eligible for WaterSure, some water companies do have other schemes available for low-income households.

⟹ Will having OCD affect my travel insurance?

Yes, but only minimally in most cases. During our research for our own travels, and for this book, what we discovered was when you declare that you have received treatment or medication for Obsessive-Compulsive Disorder, the premium is affected by a minimal amount, sometimes by just a few pence for a week's single European trip. However, the cost of the travel insurance is increased more significantly if you check the box that asks *if you are currently recommended to see a psychiatrist.*

It's important to answer this question honestly to ensure any subsequent claim is valid.

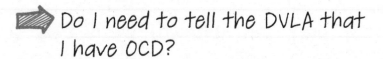

Do I need to tell the DVLA that I have OCD?

Not necessarily. The DVLA make it very clear that it depends on whether OCD impacts on your ability to drive safely.

If your OCD means you carry out regular compulsive behaviours whilst driving, then you do need to inform the DVLA. Examples of such behaviours might include compulsively checking the rear-view mirror, paying more attention to the road behind rather than the road ahead, or having to complete a set of blinking compulsions whilst driving. If the OCD causes significant concentration problems, agitation or suicidal thoughts you may also be required to notify the DVLA.

You don't need to inform the DVLA of anything if you have feelings of anxiety, terror and anguish whilst driving, providing you are driving with due care and attention to the space around you. Even if OCD has led you to obsessing over an accident or driving back over a route to check for signs of an accident.

If you're not sure if your OCD is impacting on your ability to drive safely then your therapist or doctor should be able to advise you. It's also worth remembering that different prescription medications may affect your driving in different ways, so you should always talk to your prescribing doctor or pharmacist about how your medication might affect your driving.

If you do have to inform the DVLA, they will use the information you give them to decide if you should keep your licence and will notify you in writing of their decision. They may request additional information from a doctor or ask you to undertake an additional driving assessment before making a decision.

In other parts of the world, you will need to check with your regional/state Department of Motor Vehicles (DMV) on their rules regarding notification of medical conditions.

➡ Can a person with a diagnosis of OCD receive social care from a local authority?

For some people, OCD can impact on their ability to function to the point where they may need practical help and support at home. In these cases, social care services can help.

Social care covers a wide range of activities to help people live independently. It can include 'personal care', such as support for washing, dressing, toileting or shopping, for example. Although social care services are provided by your local authority, you may have to pay for it subject to a financial and needs assessment.

If you think you might be eligible you can get more information or make a self-referral through your local authority website.

Diagnosing OCD

'Is this OCD?' is perhaps the most common question we get asked in our work. In this chapter, we will explore questions about diagnosing OCD, and offer some practical advice for how to talk about the often sensitive subject of this condition.

 ## Do online self-assessment questionnaires tell me if I have OCD or not?

Unfortunately, there are many different types of online OCD tests circling the internet. You know the type – the ones we see too often as we scroll through social media. Some of those tests are flippant and intended to be humorous, whereas others are genuinely intended to be a serious self-diagnostic tool. You can even find such tests on some OCD websites.

Whenever we're struggling with OCD, it's natural to seek clarity, and because the online quizzes are relatively quick and instant, we can understand why people might be tempted to want to seek instant answers.

The problem with this is a computer can't capture your emotions and feelings, and the online questionnaires do a relatively poor job of that too. In our opinion, even the intended serious online tests can be unreliable and should not be taken as any kind of factual guide that a person might be suffering from OCD. For this reason, if you are in any doubt about your diagnosis of OCD, please always consult a trained health professional.

How do I get a formal diagnosis?

For common OCD symptoms, sometimes a doctor may be able to give you a diagnosis, however, in most cases you'll need to be referred to a trained mental health specialist – usually a psychiatrist. They will spend some time talking to you about your problems during a meeting called an 'assessment' before the health professional will make a formal diagnosis. The assessment will ask you about the problems you are experiencing, how long you have had them, how they make you feel and the impact they have on your life.

Although a formal diagnosis can be helpful to understand the problem and give answers to people's experiences with this condition, depending on where you live, it isn't necessarily needed to access psychological therapy. The most important thing is the treatment itself, with or without a diagnosis.

However, for children and young people, a formal diagnosis can be extremely beneficial to ensure that children's mental health services offer the correct treatment, and schools offer additional help where necessary and appropriate. Some parents have expressed concern about their child being labelled with a diagnosis of OCD early in life, but most parents have felt the diagnosis was ultimately beneficial to help them access appropriate health and education support services.

To summarize, accessing a formal diagnosis for OCD can only come from a suitably trained health professional, and the first step to access that would usually be to speak to your doctor.

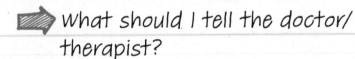# What should I tell the doctor/therapist?

The important thing to remember about therapists is that they have usually heard it all before. Just think about how many patients they have treated, and how often they hear about other people's taboo intrusive thoughts. Even if the therapist has never heard of a symptom specifically similar to yours before, remember that OCD presents slightly differently for everyone, so CBT can be adapted to your individual difficulties.

Therapists should essentially be unshockable, and they should react in a way to normalize the thoughts you find so distressing. A good therapist will naturally find a way to help you to feel comfortable in sharing your obsessions with them, by creating a non-judgemental environment for you to do so.

If your OCD involves harm-related thoughts, whilst we encourage you to be honest about your OCD, it's helpful to emphasize to the health professional that your thoughts are just that – involuntary thoughts. They are the opposite of what we actually want and intend to do and are not in line with our values and what we believe. If you're still concerned, you could tell the health professional "I have thoughts similar to those mentioned in the 'NICE Guidelines for the treatment of OCD'".

Telling the doctor is a little bit different because they aren't as experienced in talking about OCD, and they may not have the knowledge in understanding certain aspects of it. In this case, if you are sharing your obsessions with your doctor, you might want to word it differently to the way you would word it with a therapist. For example, it might be best to tell them you have been struggling with what could possibly be OCD, and the suspected obsessions are related to harm. You could then go on to mention that you have read that this is a completely normal theme to experience, and that upon research you have learned that you would benefit from some therapeutic help.

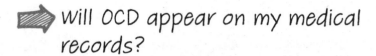 ## Will OCD appear on my medical records?

Usually, any health condition someone is diagnosed or treated for is recorded in your medical or health records. Some people are often reluctant to have OCD appear on their medical records; this could be due to many reasons, but it's often due to the fear of the potential impact on future career plans, or the negative impact on premiums for life or travel insurance.

It's possible that those concerns may never become a reality or a problem for you through life, but what we can say is there is most likely to be a problem if OCD is left untreated.

Untreated OCD could potentially get worse and prevent you from pursuing the career you want or even working at all, and it could prevent you from leading a happy and fulfilled life.

It all depends on what is important to you as an individual. However, we both believe that the positives of good treatment outweigh the negatives of having OCD on medical records.

Treatment for OCD

The good news is that despite how debilitating Obsessive-Compulsive Disorder is, it's treatable. Simply knowing that it's possible to overcome OCD can give someone the motivation to keep fighting this agonizing disorder.

Finding information about treatment for OCD can be difficult because although the internet has lots of resources, it's hard to be sure which ones are genuinely reliable. On top of that, the guidelines for accessing treatment, and what treatment looks like, can vary depending on what country you live in. This can leave people feeling confused whilst frantically searching for answers in what feels like a rabbit warren full of different information.

Within this chapter, we will break down different therapeutic approaches – which ones are evidence-based and recommended as the most effective treatment, and other commonly asked questions related to treatment for Obsessive-Compulsive Disorder.

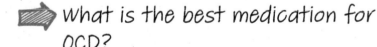 What is the best medication for OCD?

Generally speaking, the recommended type of medication used in the treatment of OCD will be a type of anti-depressant medication called Selective Serotonin Reuptake Inhibitors, most commonly referred to as SSRIs. There are currently several different types of SSRIs prescribed in the UK, which can sometimes leave people confused as to which type is best for them.

Other medications are also sometimes used alongside SSRIs or instead of SSRIs if a person has failed to respond.

For almost two decades we have been asked the question, 'Which is the best medication to take for OCD?' and our answer has sadly remained the same. Unfortunately, no matter how much we all want it, there is no magic pill that we can take that will make OCD go away, or any one medication that works for all of us.

Our individual response to medication is as unique as our bodies and experiences with OCD. If you imagine a support group room with ten attendees, all on the same brand and dosage of medication, there will most likely be ten different responses. Some may have responded well, and it helped the symptoms, some might have found the medication took the edge off sightly, whereas others might have found that the intensity of the thoughts got worse.

In essence, taking medication for OCD will be what we call 'trial-and-error' with different dosages and different brands of medications until you find the perfect fit for you. Always consult your prescribing GP or psychiatrist before changing dosage or withdrawing from the medication.

Do I have to take medication to treat OCD?

No, not at all. The health guidelines for the treatment of OCD in the UK are very clear that health professionals should take into account a patient's treatment preference when treating OCD. Those same guidelines go on to say that the treatment offered should be a choice between medication or psychological therapeutic treatment, certainly initially. You don't need to take medication first in order to be offered therapy, even if people have sometimes been told this.

Whilst neither of us are anti-medication, neither of us have used medication in our treatment. That was simply our preference, and both of us were open to medication being introduced later if it was needed.

We encourage everybody to be open to taking medication if you feel it's the right decision for you. There is no shame or weakness in needing it, and it can often be a helpful tool or treatment that supports you in your recovery journey.

Ultimately you have to make the choice that feels right for you.

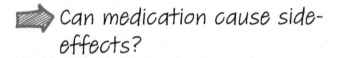 ## Can medication cause side-effects?

All medications have potential side-effects; however, this doesn't necessarily mean everyone will experience them. We are all different; we all have different bodies and tolerances to different medications and dosages.

Two people could be offered the exact same type and dosage of medication and one might experience negative side-effects, whilst the other might experience only positive changes as a result of taking the medication.

It's important to ask your prescribing doctor what the potential side-effects are, so you are aware of how you might feel, and can make your decision whilst being fully equipped with all of the information you need to know.

If you decide medication is the right path for you, until you start taking that medication, you won't know if you will have any side-effects at all. It's important to discuss any concerns and ask any questions you have before making your decision.

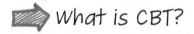 What is CBT?

Cognitive Behavioural Therapy, most commonly referred to as CBT, is a form of talking therapy. Unlike many other talking therapies, like counselling for example, it's more structured and tailored around the individuals 'here and now' problems and includes practical behavioural exercises. CBT treatment is a short-term therapy, lasting weeks and months rather than years.

CBT tackles OCD by looking at how we think, which is the cognition part (C), how this affects what we do, which is the behaviour (B), and how we feel both emotionally and physically. The treatment aims to guide us into exploring other ways of thinking and how this might affect the way we behave. CBT is based on the concept that our thoughts, feelings, and actions are all interconnected, and that negative thoughts and feelings can trap you in a vicious cycle.

The principal aim of CBT is to provide us with the tools and knowledge to become our own therapists, and practise what we know persistently so we are able to work towards recovery from Obsessive-Compulsive Disorder. Despite some myths stating that there is often a 'last chance' to get better, there are no limits to how many times someone can try CBT.

If someone has tried CBT multiple times with limited success, it should be known that this is a completely normal experience for many people with OCD, and it's important we normalize this experience to prevent people from thinking they could be 'treatment resistant', or that they are 'too unwell' to make any progress. Just because someone has experienced limited success with one therapist, it doesn't mean they won't progress with a different one. We are all different, and a therapist that has provided someone with a positive experience with CBT might not provide a different person the same experience. Take driving instructors, for example – they all teach the same information, however sometimes if we have been working with an instructor for some time with little progress, we might find that if we change the instructor, we learn the methods in a different way which suits us better.

➡️ What is ERP?

Exposure Response Prevention, most commonly referred to as ERP, is a type of therapy that encourages a person to face their fears and let obsessive thoughts occur without following them with compulsions.

The **Exposure** aspect of the therapy refers to confronting items and situations that cause anxiety, whilst the **Response Prevention aspect** refers to making a choice not to carry out a compulsion after the exposure.

The objective of the therapy is to see that the uncomfortable feelings will eventually go away, even if you don't perform a compulsion. Fundamentally it's about facing and proactively encouraging the unpleasant intrusive thoughts and feelings, rather than avoiding or trying to 'neutralize' them by carrying out a compulsion.

Although ERP will always be anxiety-provoking and challenging, a person will begin with situations that cause anxiety they are able to tolerate. After the first few times they will find that their anxiety does not climb as high or last as long. They will then move on to more difficult exposure exercises in their hierarchy ladder.

This is something I (Ashley) found with my own experiences of carrying out difficult exposure exercises. I had to proactively carry out the exposure alongside the therapist. It empowered me to have the confidence to repeat it daily on my own, and each day the level of anxiety became that little bit less until after a few days the anxiety was barely noticeable.

As the anxiety occurs after an exposure exercise, some people will choose to sit with the anxiety and resist any urges to carry out a compulsion, whilst others will try and carry on with their day to help them refocus but not avoiding triggers or thoughts.

Some people report no matter how frequently they carry out exposure exercises the anxiety remains high and doesn't change or go down. In these situations, it's worth talking to your therapist – it could be that you are subconsciously carrying out a neutralizing compulsion, so the fear level remains high.

Whilst we both appreciate and encourage the use of ERP within OCD treatment, we also appreciate the value and importance of addressing and understanding what drives our compulsions through Cognitive Behavioural Therapy (CBT) alongside ERP.

What is the difference between CBT and ERP

CBT is based on the concept that your thoughts, feelings, physical sensations and actions are interconnected and that if we change one of these, we can alter all the others. CBT tackles OCD by looking at how we think, which is the cognition part (C), how this affects what we do, which is the behaviour (B), and how we feel both emotionally and physically. **ERP** is a type of therapy that encourages a person to face their fears and let obsessive thoughts occur without following them with compulsions.

Most research suggests very little difference between CBT and ERP alone in treating OCD short term, however, some research does suggest that potentially CBT could have a better long-term benefit.

Ultimately which therapy you choose is about finding the right approach for you. Whilst we both appreciate the value of and encourage the use of ERP within OCD treatment, we also appreciate the value and importance of addressing understanding what drives our compulsions through Cognitive Behavioural Therapy (CBT) with ERP. We certainly feel one of the significant benefits of working with CBT was the change in thinking about our problems, which then allowed us to feel able to confront the OCD triggers through ERP. We would always recommend the best treatment approach to be a combination of both approaches, CBT with ERP.

➡️ Why do we do ERP?

Being asked to face your fears is perhaps one of the bravest aspects of doing ERP treatment and is where the approach of a therapist is most valuable. A therapist should help a person understand the cognitive reasons behind an exercise and encourage them to face the challenges.

A person should begin confronting fears that cause anxiety they are able to tolerate, so that they can build confidence and work towards some feared situations that are more anxiety inducing. After the first few times, they should find that their anxiety does not climb as high and does not last as long. Generally, people find exposure exercises are not as difficult as they thought they would be, and their anxiety fades away quicker than they imagined.

Successful ERP, in our experience, only happens once we have looked at our thoughts and worries and have addressed the misinterpretations that we have placed on them. Effective ERP should also lead to 'habituation'; this is where a person with OCD will learn that nothing bad happens when they stop performing their compulsive behaviours.

➡️ What is anti-OCD?

'Anti-OCD' is a phrase you may hear sometimes, and whilst it's not a clinical term with any official meaning, it can be a helpful term to understand.

If you haven't heard of the term anti-OCD yet, let us explain. An anti-OCD response to a thought is basically, in the most simplistic way possible, going against the OCD grain. As the name suggests, being anti-OCD means doing the exact opposite of what OCD wants you to do, or even by going much further than that when you can.

For example, let's say your OCD is triggered by someone telling you that mobile phones hold more germs than toilet seats do. This could trigger the intrusive thought, 'What if my phone is contaminated and I contaminate myself or others?' There are then three possible responses to this:

- OCD way

- non-OCD way (Average Response)

- anti-OCD way

OCD might want you to anti-bac your phone, the non-OCD way is to do nothing, but an anti-OCD response might be to, for example, lick the phone screen. In order to be able to achieve an average response, we have to do the anti-OCD response to reach this goal. The illustration below perhaps best highlights this theory:

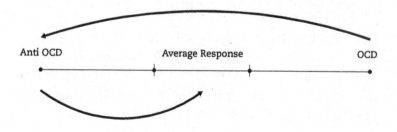

Anti OCD   Average Response   OCD

If an intrusive thought makes you feel quite triggered, and more vulnerable to OCD taking over than usual, question what the anti-OCD response might be. Challenge it in that moment to nip it in the bud and if you feel able to, implement the anti-OCD response. By behaving anti-OCD, it can support us to remain in recovery and in control of our behaviours. If you're not sure what your anti-OCD exposure exercise will be, talk to your therapist and ask them to help you work towards that.

Does hypnotherapy help?

Hypnotherapy is a type of complementary therapy that uses hypnosis, which is an altered state of consciousness and involves being put in a deeply relaxed state. Hypnosis is widely promoted as a treatment for various long-term conditions including OCD, and for breaking certain habits. This is despite the fact that there's no strong evidence to support these uses.

We don't recommend the use of hypnotherapy to treat OCD, but we have had experiences of sufferers using it to help manage their anxiety. Therefore, although some people use it as a management tool, we wouldn't recommend using it to treat the disorder because it isn't an evidence-based treatment for OCD.

If you do decide to give hypnotherapy a try, always check the credentials of the hypnotherapist and check if they belong to an appropriate accreditation body.

Does EMDR help?

EMDR stands for Eye Movement Desensitization and Reprocessing. Whilst it's not formally recommended for the treatment of OCD, and there remains limited research evidence to support its use at this time, we are seeing an increase in local therapy services sending patients for EMDR to treat their OCD.

EMDR was specifically created to help people with difficult traumatic memories, including people experiencing Post Traumatic Stress Disorder (PTSD). EMDR combines talking to a therapist about traumatic experiences with a technique where you make rapid rhythmic eye movements while recalling traumatic events to help you process them. The rapid eye movements are intended to create a similar effect to the way your brain processes memories and experiences while you're sleeping.

If your therapist recommends EMDR, a good question is to ask why. Is it because they genuinely believe EMDR is right for you, especially if you have other problems that you need help with, or is it because of their own limitations with OCD/CBT?

Whilst neither of us would recommend EMDR over Cognitive Behavioural Therapy (CBT) to treat OCD, that's not to say it can't help and there may be some benefit if that person has experienced some form of trauma. In those cases, EMDR may be the right treatment approach initially.

 Does mindfulness help with OCD?

Whilst we don't recommend mindfulness as a treatment for OCD, some people say they find a benefit in helping them feel calmer and less anxious to better manage their day-to-day wellbeing. We would perhaps consider mindfulness a tool to compliment the recommended psychological therapy for OCD, rather than replacing it.

Mindfulness is a meditation technique which has roots in Buddhism and meditation, but you don't have to be spiritual to try it. It involves focussing on the present moment, without judgement to improve self-awareness and cope better with difficult thoughts and feelings.

➡️ what is a hierarchy?

Waiting for therapy to start can be frustrating, but that's not to say you can't do something in preparation, and it could be helpful for you to create your OCD hierarchy. This hierarchy is essentially a list of your feared situations ranked in order of your most anxiety provoking at the top, down to the least anxiety provoking at the bottom.

This is a great exercise to help you start to think about your OCD and how it impacts on the different areas of your life. Don't worry if the list is a few items or a few pages – for most of us the first time we do this it's scarily several pages long.

The idea is the hierarchy is used to guide you through therapy and hopefully help you measure some level of progression as you tackle your OCD. It's also sometimes called a ladder hierarchy, which is a good way to visualize it; a ladder with lots of steps, each step representing your OCD fears.

Recovery

OCD

Whilst tackling the item at the top of the list is the end goal, in most cases that will simply be too scary to tackle either alone or in therapy. We both believe it is usually helpful to start with items that are ranked lower. The point is to start with something that makes you anxious, but not so anxious that you can't reach it and gain some confidence to tackle the next step. As you progress you will find that you should start jumping multiple steps up your ladder.

The illustration will help visualize this process. Eventually each step you take could lead you to reaching your therapy goal.

You continue this step-by-step process until you have met your therapy/recovery goals. This usually means reaching and feeling more confident to tackle the highest item on your OCD ladder hierarchy.

Remember, how quickly you get to the top step doesn't matter – all that matters is you reach as high up as you can, when you can. Don't underestimate the importance of using your hierarchy and taking small steps – they can lead to higher places.

How to Access Treatment

As complicated and terrifying as living with OCD is, accessing treatment can be equally as complicated and terrifying. We have both experienced struggling with the system when trying to access OCD treatment. We hope our answers within this chapter will bring clarity and direction to help you make that next step to a life without OCD.

➡️ Do you need a therapist to overcome OCD?

Whilst we do know of people who have worked their way through self-help resources without a therapist, we are both enthusiastic about the positives that therapeutic intervention with a therapist has on the recovery process. It might sound straightforward to read self-help books, educate ourselves through presentations and lectures and apply these learnings to our own problems. However, a therapist is one of the most powerful tools that exists to help someone overcome OCD.

A therapist can help us to unravel some of the misconceptions we place on our thoughts, and they often pick up on cognitive problems we have no idea we are even struggling with. Both of us have had experiences with therapists where we have had lightbulb moments after years of being confused by our own feelings and why we were behaving the way we did. We both strongly feel that without those lightbulb moments we wouldn't have been able to make the choice to challenge certain aspects of OCD.

It's possible that without a therapist, you could fail to recognize a thought process that is much more obvious to a therapist. Therefore, whilst working through it alone could help you, the therapist could take that one step further and help you to recover.

As we all know, it can be quite terrifying to try behavioural experiments and unravel the cognitive problems we are experiencing. Therefore, a therapist is also a supportive figure who can give proactive encouragement when we are working through difficult aspects of treatment.

In summary, we aren't saying self-help resources aren't useful in the recovery process, because they absolutely are. However, in our opinion they are best used as one of the many tools we can use alongside therapeutic intervention.

➡ How do I access treatment?

Accessing treatment will vary, not just across countries around the world, but even across the UK. We will try and guide you within this question, however, we recommend checking with local OCD charities or appropriate health service websites for advice on how to access treatment in your area.

Here in the UK, the great news is that treatment for OCD is freely available for eligible UK residents through the National Health Service (NHS). Access to treatment will depend on which part of the UK you live in. If you live in Wales, Scotland, or Northern Ireland, you will nearly always need to visit your GP. There can be some regional variations, so if you're unsure you can check with your GP or local NHS mental health service website. Your GP can make a referral to your local community mental health team (CMHT) for psychological treatment and prescribe medication should that be required.

In England access is slightly different, although you can still see your GP should you wish to, and you may need to eventually in order to access NHS services that specialize in treating anxiety/OCD. Initially and often the quickest route to accessing treatment is to self-refer to your local NHS therapy service. This can be done without needing to see your GP. Each part of England has its own IAPT service (pronounced i-apt). IAPT stands for Improving Access to Psychological Therapies, often rebranded to a local regional service name, such as Let's Talk Wellbeing or Healthy Minds.

You can search for your local IAPT service by typing 'Find a psychological therapies service' into a search engine or by contacting an OCD charity who will help you find your local service. You can then usually self-refer by completing an online form on their website or by calling and telling them you want to 'self-refer for CBT'. You will initially be offered a 60–90-minute telephone assessment, and following that be placed on a waiting list for CBT.

In other parts of the world access to treatment will vary subject to region, and may require self-funding of a therapist – something we call in the UK, 'private treatment'. Regardless of where you are in the world, for those with health insurance the cost of that treatment may be covered, but you will need to check with the therapist that they accept your health insurance.

There are many factors to consider when paying for access to a therapist, in addition to practical matters such as cost and location, although the rise of online therapy can help mitigate location concerns. It's also important to find the 'right' therapist. The right therapist is someone who you will feel comfortable working with, and most importantly, who is knowledgeable and experienced in successfully treating OCD using CBT (including ERP).

Let's not pull any punches. You don't need to even search online for OCD therapists – social media advertising algorithms show them as you're simply browsing. The problem with this is that many are simply not suitably qualified and very expensive, which is partly why they are advertising. It's also important not to be persuaded by therapists with active social media accounts, mass follow counts or seemingly free-flowing testimonials from other sufferers – from our work we know that sometimes all is not what it seems.

So how do you find the right therapist? Local OCD charities and doctor/health service websites may have local recommendations or advice on finding a therapist. If you do happen to stumble across a therapist website online or a friend recommends someone, the most important criteria when searching for a private therapist or doctor is that they are accredited with the appropriate professional body, and that they have a good understanding of OCD and CBT (including ERP).

Whichever therapist you choose, you should also ask about cost so there are no hidden surprises. Be wary of any therapist that demands payment up front for multiple sessions. We recommend you pay for one session at a time, at least initially, until you know you can work with that therapist. Remember, when paying privately you can end the session at any time, and you don't need to give a reason – it's your money, you get to choose and decide. Some key points that may be helpful to remember:

- You are entitled to ask questions. The OCD charities will have a list of questions you can ask a therapist to help you establish if the therapist is right for you. If the therapist is reluctant to answer your questions, then you should probably look elsewhere.

- Don't be afraid to look for a different therapist if after the first couple of sessions you don't feel this therapist is the right one for you. That's nobody's fault – sometimes we need to move on if we don't feel we can effectively communicate with our current therapist.

- Do they offer a free introductory brief conversation over the telephone to allow you to decide whether you can work together? They should offer you at least a 10 minute chat.

- Not all but some therapists may be able to offer reduced rates for people on low incomes.

- If you're unable to make an appointment (as we all know OCD can sometimes make that happen!), do they charge for missed appointments?

OCD is a complex illness, so it's important to choose the right therapist to help you overcome OCD, rather than a therapist that is a little bit cheaper and a little closer to where we live. Choosing the right therapist can, in the long run, prove more cost effective, even if it means paying a little more per session and travelling a little further.

In summary, finding the right therapist is a challenge, and we hope our answer helps empower you more than scare you. Most importantly, don't worry. Most therapists genuinely are there to try and help you. If you do find a therapist but you're not sure if they are suitable, email one of the OCD charities who will be able to check and advise you if they're suitability accredited.

Which is better – an NHS therapist or a private therapist?

The best therapist for you is the one who helps you begin and move forward along your recovery journey, regardless of whether or not that therapist is NHS or private! To illustrate this point – and for clarity – one of us has been helped most by NHS therapists and the other by a private therapist. You can experience good and bad treatment both privately and within the NHS, and a therapist's ability to successfully treat OCD should be judged on their individual suitability.

There are some fantastic and some not-so-good NHS therapists, just as there are also some fantastic and some not-so-good private therapists. There are also some globally respected OCD specialists that work exclusively through the NHS. Regardless of whether you access treatment privately or within the NHS, one great question to ask your therapist the first time you meet them is 'What experience do you have in successfully treating OCD?'

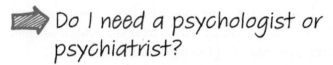 Do I need a psychologist or psychiatrist?

In essence, you could work with either, or sometimes we may work alongside both a psychiatrist, psychologist and/or other mental health professionals simultaneously depending on the level of care we need. All of whom will be working collaboratively to help us.

For example, a therapist (who may be a clinical psychologist) will provide us with our psychological therapy (CBT including ERP) and a psychiatrist (who will be a medical doctor) might work with us to prescribe any medication.

A simplistic way to think about the difference between psychiatry and psychology is that psychiatry refers to a specific branch of medicine that focuses on the causes, prevention, diagnosis and treatment of mental health conditions. Psychology is the study of people, how they think, how they act, react and interact and uses talking therapy approaches, such as CBT.

➡ How many therapy sessions will I need?

It will always be difficult to say how many treatment sessions we will need. For some people therapy can make a difference quickly, however for others it might not work immediately and may take many months.

When accessing therapy, it can be helpful to give yourself a rough timeline, because not only is never-ending therapy unhelpful, it can be costly too. A good benchmark is about 8–12 hours (one hour a week), and if by around that time you're not seeing *any* progress at all, you should be asking questions about whether the therapy is working. Don't be afraid to find a different therapist if you come to the conclusion that it isn't.

Some people have stayed with the same therapist for a year or longer because they like them and feel they can talk to them. Whilst that is important, it's worth remembering the reason we first went to therapy was to overcome OCD, so that should remain our goal and we need an effective therapist to help us to achieve that.

Treatment Myths

Reaching out for help and going to therapy can be a big decision for some, so when it doesn't work it's frustrating. This is made even harder by commonly repeated myths about treatment, which can sometimes be a barrier to accessing further treatment and getting the help and support they need.

In this chapter, we set out to answer some of the myths that surround therapy and, most importantly, we want to use this introduction to tell you that no matter how old you are, how much previous treatment you may have already had or regardless of the severity your OCD, if you're still experiencing Obsessive-Compulsive Disorder then **YOU** deserve treatment just as much as anybody else.

What if treatment doesn't help?

If treatment doesn't help, it could be because of a number of factors. The first suggestion we would make is to question if this therapist is the right therapist for you. This doesn't necessarily mean the therapist is a bad therapist (of course it could mean this), but maybe their approach isn't one you respond well to. In which case, finding a different therapist might be the best option for you.

Secondly, does your therapist know the extent of your fears and behaviours? We know it's hard to be completely honest with a therapist. OCD is so embarrassing to talk about, it's scary to think what their reaction might be and being honest about your problems is extremely challenging. However, the more information the therapist has, the more they can understand the problem. Try not to be hard on yourself if you haven't been completely honest with your therapist – this isn't necessarily your fault. It could be that you didn't feel it was an environment which enabled you to be completely transparent, and a different therapist might ask the right questions and create an environment that allows you to more easily open up and be honest.

If you find you have exhausted all other options of local treatment, and you still find that treatment isn't helping, don't give up. This doesn't mean you are 'treatment resistant', or that this was your last chance at overcoming OCD. It might mean that seeing an OCD specialist is the right path for you. A therapist doesn't have to be specialized in OCD to be good at treating it, however, specialists have a lot more experience, and they might be able to unravel certain aspects of your experiences with OCD that could have been previously missed in treatment.

Remember, there is no limit on the number of times a person can try therapy. We know it can be exhausting if you have had to try treatment numerous times with little recovery progress, but for some people it can take a few attempts. This is normal, and it doesn't mean you won't recover.

➡️ Am I treatment resistant?

This is a term we both hate, and here's why. Treatment resistant means that regardless of what situation you are in, what type of therapist you see, or how much you try, you simply cannot progress with treatment, and you will always live in your current state of distress with OCD. This isn't necessarily true.

One of the main problems with this term is that it can prevent someone seeking further help after experiencing therapy that hasn't proven to be initially successful. This is usually down to the fact that they feel it would be pointless working towards a goal that doesn't exist for them.

It's extremely common to have to try therapy multiple times before making any great progress with recovery, but if someone thought this meant they were resistant to treatment completely, would they attempt to try again? Or would they accept they will never progress, and that this is something they will have to live with every day for the rest of their lives? We think the latter!

We don't believe anyone is treatment resistant. We are aware that some people have comorbidities which make their progressions with therapy and treatment more difficult, with extra barriers and difficulties. We know that some people might need certain adaptations in their therapy, sometimes due to their comorbidities. However, this doesn't mean that it's impossible to make any progressions with therapy for OCD in the future. Any progress made, even the smallest of steps, is showing that a person is responding to treatment. Next time the progression might be an even bigger step.

It's extremely hard for us to get better if we believe that we never will.

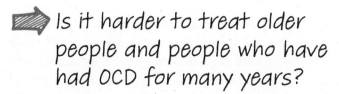 Is it harder to treat older people and people who have had OCD for many years?

No, not necessarily, but for all of us, regardless of age, recovery is subject to the person accessing the right therapy and therapist. The right therapist with experience in treating OCD will help us make sense of our OCD problems and begin to challenge them.

For someone with decades of OCD fears, worries and emotions it would not be unexpected if treatment took a little longer for some older people, but there is no reason to believe that treating

OCD is harder for them. We once worked with a patient in their eighties who had OCD for over 60 years. That person worked with an OCD specialist for several months and made a successful recovery.

Regardless of the patient's age, any work needed to challenge behaviours could be hindered by any mobility issues or physical disabilities, so could require a little more patience and flexibility by the therapist to adapt therapy accordingly.

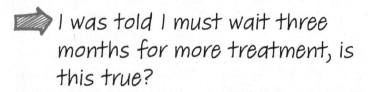 I was told I must wait three months for more treatment, is this true?

No, that's not true. No person should wait longer than necessary for treatment. When we reach out for psychological therapy, we will be offered a 'course' of treatment sessions. A course will usually range from 8 to 12 individual one hour therapy sessions. If at the end of a course of therapy our OCD is still a problem, we should be offered more therapy, either with the same therapist or passed (sometimes called 'stepped up') to another more experienced therapist.

However, we know that it's not uncommon for a person to be told by some therapy services that they must wait three to six months before they can request more sessions, sometimes with reasons like 'to give therapy time to work'. This is simply not the case, and NHS England have been very clear that NHS therapy services are expected to follow the OCD treatment recommendations in the national treatment guidelines, which is clear further treatment should be explored.

You don't have to wait for three months before you can ask for more therapy. If your OCD is still impacting on your life, then you deserve and are entitled to request more therapy without having to wait a period of time.

We are both of the belief that the therapy you are offered should only end when you have made sufficient recovery to be able to say that your OCD is no longer impacting significantly on your life.

➡️ Should therapy only take place in the therapist's office?

This is not straightforward to answer, because since the pandemic we have seen a rise in the use of online and hybrid therapy. Online therapy is conducted through video technology platforms like Microsoft Teams or Zoom, and hybrid is a mix of online and traditional face-to-face. The research evidence will show in the future if OCD treatment is better face-to-face or online, but we are both of the belief that some level of face-to-face therapy could be beneficial for some if OCD requires in-person support when conducting difficult exposure exercises. In all likelihood, the hybrid model will almost certainly be the perfect compromise for treatment moving forward.

However, this then brings us to another aspect to this question when talking about face-to-face therapy and difficult exposure exercises. In some cases, such exercises will be required at a patient's home or being around substances or people that might trigger a person's intrusive thoughts and obsessions. In this case, in an ideal world a therapist would arrange to carry out some of the therapy sessions on location. However, due to limited therapy service resources this is often unlikely to happen. You may need to request that your therapist agrees to on-location therapy if you feel that would help you, although you may need to move the day/time of the session to facilitate this. If this can't be facilitated, and you feel empowered enough to try the exposure, you could arrange to do so with a supportive family member or friend the first time, and then arrange for the therapy session that same day or the next morning to talk though how you felt.

This brings us on to the question: 'Should we work at therapy ourselves between sessions and should the therapy sessions with the therapist only happen in the therapists office?' We will share our thoughts to help guide you.

A common myth is that the only work a person has to do in order to get better, is during that one hour a week they spend in the therapist's office. However, the therapeutic techniques that we learn should become integrated into our everyday life in-between therapy sessions and post therapy.

In summary, the location of where we have therapy will vary, depending on what is right for each of us; online, face-to-face, on location or a hybrid of all these.

Does overcoming OCD mean not having intrusive thoughts?

Definitely not. Intrusive thoughts are not the problem, despite what OCD wants us to believe. Neither are they unique to OCD because everyone experiences sad, scary, disgusting or violent intrusive thoughts from time to time. It's part of being human and it's impossible to stop them from happening.

Recovery from OCD is about changing the way we respond to intrusive thoughts and the relationship we have with them, not stopping them all together. In fact, what you will find is that the harder you try to stop intrusive thoughts from happening, the more you end up thinking about them. It's like if you push down on a ball under water – the harder you try, the more aggressively it will pop back up to hit us in the face!

Thoughts are just thoughts, and the aim of recovery is to learn not to apply meaning to them or react to them. It's about understanding that they will happen, and that's OK.

OCD Self-help

Many of you reading our book today will be doing so having not previously read anything else about OCD, and we hope we can take away some of the myriad of questions that we both had when we first started out on this journey to understand and overcome our respective OCD.

We hope that collectively our book and all these other fantastic resources enable you to feel inspired and empowered to make positive choices in managing your OCD until such time as you can start to work towards your recovery.

What can I do whilst on a several-month-long treatment waiting list?

When you are suffering with Obsessive-Compulsive Disorder and you are on a lengthy waiting list for treatment, it can be hard to know what to do in the meantime to cope. Not only that, but it can be extremely scary knowing that although you feel you have hit rock bottom, there isn't any help available for some time. There are a few things you can do to support yourself and tread the water until you can access therapeutic help, so we thought we would go through some of these here.

One activity we recommend is reading. We know sometimes it can feel like people throw a handful of different blogs, books and information at you all at once, but it does help. If you feel overwhelmed with too much information, set yourself a schedule of dedicated reading time each day/week. Knowledge is power, and the more we know about OCD – why we are feeling the way we are, or behaving the way we do – the better. When it comes to learning about overcoming OCD, although we might not be able to implement the learnings ourselves without any treatment, it's helpful to know what we need to do, even if we can't do it right now. Not only does this prepare us for what to expect, but it also reminds us that eventually we will be doing something which will make our lives better again. There are also online presentations and webinars if you find that hearing someone speak is easier than reading the information.

We also recommend talking to someone else who knows how it feels to suffer from OCD. There are often online support groups and forums available where you can confide in people who understand your journey more than anyone else. It can be lonely suffering from OCD when you feel misunderstood.

Last but not least, find activities that can help you to refocus. Whether that be walking in the countryside, doing something creative like drawing or painting, baking, running or anything that you find therapeutic or a helpful form of escapism. Refocusing isn't a long-term solution, as eventually it could become avoidance if we never face our fears, but it's certainly helpful in the in the wait for treatment, or as an addition to it.

And finally, talk. Tell your loved ones that you are struggling. A friend, family member, house mate, colleague. Talk. OCD thrives off fear, and when we hide away from talking about OCD, it becomes more powerful. That feeling of relief when you have finally got something off your chest which has been weighing you down is your step forward, and OCD's step back.

What are the best books for OCD?

There are many books about OCD written by people from all walks of life. Some books will tell the story of a person who has also experienced OCD, which may offer great comfort to you, knowing somebody else has similar experiences to your own. Other books are written by health professionals which primarily focus on what OCD is and about the research. And then there are self-help books which are designed to guide you to help yourself. Self-help books are usually written by specialists in the field of OCD, and as when seeking a private therapist, the best books are in our experience those written by suitability qualified health professionals.

Self-help books don't always serve to improve our day-to-day functioning, particularly at the start of our journey prior to psychological therapy. That's not to say they can't be helpful, but for some people the books are more effective as a companion alongside therapy, or post therapy when we are working towards recovery without a therapist anymore.

Just as all therapists have different styles and approaches, the same can be said for books, so sometimes you may have to read several of them to find the right one to guide you along your self-help journey. Sometimes it may not be one book but chunks of text from several books that you find helpful and useful. The OCD charities will have a list of recommended books.

Will talking in a support group make my OCD worse?

It shouldn't do. Generally, support groups (and forums) help people feel supported, understood and less alone with their OCD symptoms. They can help people feel connected to others who understand how OCD can make you feel, and they offer you an addition to your support network with the opportunity to get to know other people who have a level of understanding of your struggles.

In our experience, what makes a support group powerful is being around different people at different stages of recovery. Some people attending support groups have only recently been diagnosed or have only recently started to experience OCD. Some people might be a lot further along in their recovery journey, offering their personal advice on how to keep going through the distress OCD causes. A dynamic group like this can help people learn from each other and support each other through current and new challenges.

It's not unheard of to find support groups triggering, but in our experience, it's rare. It's important that the person running the support group maintains a level of positivity, reminding people that recovery is possible and offering them the relevant tools and information for whatever they are struggling with. A competent support group host will acknowledge peoples' struggles and allow them the time and space to feel hurt and upset. However, they will also make sure to guide people who have lost hope by offering them the tools to see the light at the end of the OCD tunnel.

We understand that for some people it can be quite alarming to join a support group at the beginning of their OCD journey, and hear people talk about experiences of suffering from OCD for a long period of time. It's important to understand that everyone is different – we all progress at our own pace, and focusing on your own recovery journey without comparing it to other people's is crucial. Don't feel pressured to talk in a support group if you don't yet feel ready – some people find it easier to sit and listen before they share.

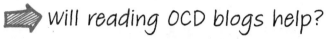 # Will reading OCD blogs help?

Absolutely! Reading stories about other people's experiences with Obsessive-Compulsive Disorder can reduce those feelings of loneliness. It's common to feel misunderstood when you are suffering from OCD, so when you read someone else's words that perfectly describe the difficulties you experience, it can make you feel more understood and less isolated.

That being said, be careful not to compare your journey to someone else's. We are all very different, and although OCD has many similarities for people who suffer from it, we also experience many differences too. People work through recovery in different ways. For some people fortunate enough to meet the right therapist the first time around, they might find themselves working towards recovery quicker than someone who hasn't been as fortunate to receive appropriate treatment yet.

As helpful and reassuring as reading other people's stories can be, be careful not to fall into the trap of just reading. At some point, in order to move forward with recovery, we have to act and challenge OCD.

Working and OCD

Whilst some people with Obsessive-Compulsive Disorder find that working is good for their mental wellbeing, others can find the condition creates added stress and challenges in the workplace.

In this chapter, we explore some of those challenges and offer practical advice and guidance to help you navigate OCD in the workplace.

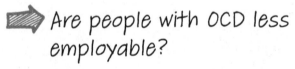

Are people with OCD less employable?

Absolutely not.

One of the misconceptions of OCD is that people are continually repeating behaviours and compulsions which makes them late for work or less productive. But for many people with OCD this could not be further from the truth, despite difficulties their problems haven't interfered with work.

That's not to say sometimes OCD can't impact on some of us in the workplace, but with an understanding employer and reasonable adjustments to help, that impact is often manageable.

Will OCD stop me working?

Unfortunately, for some people with OCD the answer to this is yes, although how long it impacts on their ability to work will vary. For others, quick treatment interventions mean a person can continue working.

If OCD does stop you working, that does not mean it will always stop you getting a job. Successful OCD treatment can lead to recovery to the point where you feel able to reach out and enjoy everything life has to offer, and for you that might include working at a job you love.

One of the people we both work with through the charity, by her own admission, said that after initially starting out working as a nurse she had since been unable to work for 15 years because of OCD and other mental health problems. During that time, she worked with her mental health services and was able to then begin a phased return to work for a few hours a week, which has subsequently become several days a week over the last 11 years. This shows that returning to work, even after many years' absence, can happen.

If you do find that you're not able to work right now or have not for a length of time, here are some practical suggestions we would recommend in case you're not already aware of them.

- Work with your local mental health service to continue challenging OCD. Remember, if OCD impacts on your life, you're entitled to more treatment.

- Check if your local mental health service offer employment support courses through their service or local mental health recovery colleges.

- You don't have to go back to work full-time straight away – it's OK to build back up with a few hours each week until you feel able to do more.

- Look into retraining opportunities through your local job centre and seek advice on writing your CV.

- Contact a local charity to enquire about volunteer work for a few hours each week – this will help your phased return back into work and add to your CV if there's been a gap in your employment history.

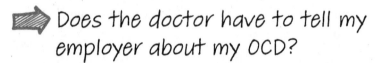

Does the doctor have to tell my employer about my OCD?

What you tell your doctor and other health professionals should remain confidential, although if they feel you're struggling they may suggest you inform your employer yourself so that they can offer you additional support. However, they must seek your permission before sharing any aspect of your health with anyone else, and the only exception to this is if they believe that you're at risk of harming yourself or someone else.

Rest assured that the doctor and therapist <u>should</u> treat your physical and mental health problems as confidential.

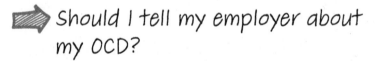

Should I tell my employer about my OCD?

If you have a mental health problem like OCD, we understand that you might not feel comfortable telling your employer about it, and that's OK. Often people have told us they worry about confidentiality in the workplace, how this may impact on their career or how they may be treated if people perceive them differently.

Ultimately, what you say and when you say it is your choice. If you're someone who has rarely experienced OCD impacting them in the workplace, you may choose not to say anything. But if you find it does and you need some additional support or time off to attend therapy, you may want to tell your employer.

If you tell your employer about OCD you are protected under the Equality Act, which means you shouldn't be discriminated against. They need to know you have a disability (OCD) and how it impacts on you at work in order to be able to make appropriate adjustments in the workplace for you.

How and when to tell your employer can be challenging, but if you're worried that they may not understand you, perhaps you could print out a page about the disorder from one of the OCD charity websites. You don't need to tell them all about the personal aspects of your OCD, but perhaps the most important thing they need to know is how it will impact you at work, therefore you could make a list in advance in case you forget an important aspect of what you want to tell them on the day you speak to them.

➡️ Are there jobs that people with OCD are more suited for?

To put it simply, no. OCD isn't a personality trait, and the people who have it are all very different. Therefore, different people with OCD will have different desires to follow their chosen career paths, just like people without it.

However, it isn't uncommon for people to believe that someone with OCD might be better at a particular, perfectionist-type job. For example, it's often misconceived that someone with OCD would be good at being an accountant, because they would create a 'perfectionist' approach in their role and be sure to check the numbers repetitively. One of the many problems with this belief is that not only is it assuming everyone with OCD experiences checking compulsions, but it's also assuming that if a person did have checking compulsions, the OCD would definitely fixate on their job.

It's also important for us to remember that OCD doesn't bring us any positives. It isn't a helpful tool, or something that enhances our lives. Let's say someone with OCD, who is mathematically skilled, with checking and 'just right' compulsions, works as an accountant. Let's imagine the OCD has fixated on their job and the compulsions begin to creep in at work. Whilst it might sound helpful to be repetitively checking everything is correct, we must remember this is a mental health problem, and being in a state of anxiety and distress should never be a requirement to succeed in a job role. On top of that, we must remember that when it comes to OCD the solution becomes the problem. Eventually the checking is likely to escalate, taking more and more time, ultimately making someone struggle to move on to new tasks and work through deadlines.

We would recommend for you to follow your desires with your career path based on your skills, what you enjoy and what makes you who you are. We don't believe you should plan long-term goals around OCD, but you should focus instead on the career path you really want to navigate.

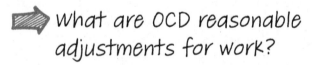 What are OCD reasonable adjustments for work?

Reasonable adjustments are changes that your employer can make to help you stay well and continue to work effectively and productively. An employer has to make reasonable adjustments for anybody with a disability and for your employer to make the adjustment they do need to know about your OCD.

However, adjustments can also be made by ourselves and there may be small changes we can make in order to better help ourselves at work. These will vary from person to person, as will the adjustments the employer will make.

Before you speak to your employer it could be helpful to think about what changes would help the difficulties you experience because of OCD, and it might be a good idea to make a list to help you to inform them of the extent of your problems. Reasonable adjustments for some could be short term, where a person is successfully working with a therapist to address those problems. For others, the OCD could mean the adjustments are more long term.

➡ I find my job makes my OCD worse – should I stop working or change jobs?

Jobs can be a source of triggers for OCD and that often leads people to change jobs to avoid those triggers. As OCD can fixate on absolutely anything, OCD left untreated typically follows us wherever we go. In other words, the compulsion of avoidance simply doesn't work. The same can be said for taking time off work. Doing this can increase the time you have to think about your worries, leaving OCD time to become more bothersome day to day.

If your job is something you have worked very hard to achieve and you found it enjoyable before OCD, you may wish to continue with it, until such time you can work with a therapist. This is where you might look into temporarily reducing your hours or changing duties as a reasonable adjustment.

For others who might not enjoy their job, and find it a stressful environment, and that it only makes fighting OCD that much harder, they might want to look into a change of profession. The most important thing to do in this situation is to figure out if the reason for leaving is because of unhappiness at work, or because OCD is the problem.

If you do decide to leave a job because of OCD, it's important to make sure that you seek treatment for OCD as soon as possible. That way you can challenge OCD and get back into the workplace with hopefully the least disruption possible.

If you're still working, but you are finding it difficult to do the work because of OCD, speak to your manager and book an appointment with your doctor as soon as you can. Talk to them about your options, be honest about the impact of work on your OCD and mental health. They may be able to offer support to help you remain in work or discuss if you need to be signed off work for a short time. During this time, it's vital to try and access therapy and work on your self-care, even if that means just recharging your batteries and refreshing your memory with therapy tools you have used previously.

Life in Recovery

Anybody who suffers because of Obsessive-Compulsive Disorder deserves to experience recovery. Recovery is so beautiful; it brings colour back to life and replaces time spent reacting compulsively with more time to live. Whilst something as simple as just leaving the house within a few minutes means very little to people without OCD, for some people in recovery from OCD it's a constant reminder of their hard work, persistence and stoicism. The ability to perform very average tasks isn't taken for granted by people in recovery, and any second spent in a moment of happiness is received with feelings of gratitude.

Although recovery can be a beautiful thing to experience, it can also leave us with an OCD-shaped hole in our lives. For some, OCD has taken so much away from them that they are left with collateral damage. This is why it's as important as ever to continue to practice what you know, and it can be helpful to have a plan in place to help you to rebuild the life you want to live.

In this chapter, we will explore questions related to recovery from OCD, including relapse prevention and how to 'stay on track'.

What should I do in recovery?

'Nature abhors a vacuum' a professor once warned at one of our OCD conferences. An often-overlooked aspect of the collateral damage of OCD is the amount of time it takes from our lives. What the professor meant by using that Aristotle quote was that should we be fortunate enough to find ourselves in recovery, we must fill that newfound space with positive actions that bring value to our lives to ensure we continue to improve our quality of life.

Recovering from OCD is not the easiest; often after undergoing treatment and the new experience of life without OCD it can be difficult to adapt to this change. The structure of our days takes on a completely different look and we're facing a new lifestyle. For some that can be exciting, but there are many unknowns and sometimes, despite the recovery, people find the unknowns harder than the OCD itself.

At first, we may be perhaps somewhat more mindful of potentially sliding into an obsessive way of thinking, especially around something that previously would have caused OCD triggers, and this can be even harder when we are also still applying therapeutic techniques into our everyday activities. This makes it even more important to have a plan that will ensure we can increase our enjoyment in life, thus ensuring we will be mentally stronger.

If you were looking for a way to experience life outside recovery, first start with discovering new hobbies, or revisiting your previously abandoned hobbies and passions. Don't be afraid to explore new passions and remember: it's OK to be happy. Don't feel guilty for enjoying yourself; after everything you have been through you deserve this happiness.

Examples of what you now have the time and mental energy to explore might include:

- making trips to visit family and friends
- travelling – locally or starting to save for that overseas destination that you can now take

- studying for that qualification you want

- changing or pursuing the career you have always wanted

- joining social groups or evening classes

- dating again or learning to date (and don't let age hold you back)

- enjoying reading books again

- starting a family

- taking on a physical challenge, like a big cycling adventure or running a marathon

- eating in restaurants

- visiting the cinema or theme parks

The list is infinite and will be individual to you, so your first job is to create your list of positive life actions you can do this year or beyond, or if that feels too much, start with this week or month. What is the one positive thing you can do for yourself this week/month that OCD previously made difficult or prevented you from doing?

When your life feels rich and satisfying, then your mental health will be strengthened, and you will be putting recovery into action. You will be living the life you want, regardless of intrusive thoughts or OCD symptoms.

We know that many of you reading this book may be at the start of your journey with OCD, so you may feel this question is not for you and you may even think it never will be. It's OK to feel like that – perhaps you could park this question for now, and place this book on your bookshelf once you finish reading it. You can always revisit this if you feel you want to at a later time.

 What is relapse prevention?

The final session of your psychological therapy can be a really positive sign that OCD is no longer impacting on your life and things have improved significantly for you. However, it's also understandably a time when people tell us they are concerned that they may lose the progress, or that their recovery journey will come to a standstill or even slip backwards, which is something commonly referred to as a relapse.

Towards the end of your psychological therapy your therapist should be helping you to create a relapse prevention plan. The aim of this is to help you refer back to what you have learned in treatment, implement those strategies and help you maintain your progress to stay well.

Don't worry – you have already demonstrated to yourself through your psychological therapy that you have the skills to help yourself recover, so the relapse prevention plan should be there to help you identify when and how to implement what you have learned. Remember, you have the skills to maintain that recovery, no matter what life throws at you.

If you do unfortunately slip, don't worry. In all probability, it will be a temporary lapse or setback, rather than a permanent relapse. Recognizing a lapse for what it is and not losing hope that things will improve again is so important – you've got this. It's also important to be kind to ourselves; being compassionate and not judging ourselves for relapsing or experiencing a setback is crucial.

If when you reach your final therapy session your therapist has not mentioned a relapse prevention plan, ask them for an additional session to help you create yours.

Does someone in recovery from OCD have to be careful not to slip into old habits?

Recovery can mean different things to different people, but we believe that being in recovery from Obsessive-Compulsive Disorder doesn't mean we are immune from ever slipping back into OCD's patterns of thinking.

If we have spent a long time reacting to intrusive thoughts a certain way, it's natural for our brains to want to react that way again. It's like if you break your leg – sure, you can recover from that. Your leg can be fixed, and you can walk again. Physio is often revisited to strengthen the leg, keep it moving and maintain the recovery process. However, there can sometimes be some nerve damage that requires you to be mindful when carrying out certain activities. We feel this is a good metaphor for recovery from OCD. We can revisit exposures and continue to implement our cognitive learnings to prevent OCD from creeping back and nipping any potential new obsessions in the bud. However, much like being mindful of certain activities with a previously broken leg, there are some things we have to be mindful of when in recovery from OCD.

Someone with no lived experience of OCD might be able to quickly google a symptom to see why they might have a headache. However, for someone who has experienced OCD – particularly someone who has previously obsessed over health symptoms – it could be riskier. The action could potentially have different consequences. The one-time google search might not be enough, and they could be at risk of slipping back into old habits.

Whilst we feel that recovery from OCD is possible and we can regain control of our own lives, we also feel that it's important to be mindful of our journey to recovery by staying awake to the possible traps and tricks, and keeping our learnings from CBT with ERP close to us. It's important to keep our new relationships with intrusive thoughts maintained by choosing to accept them and not react to them.

To conclude this question, we think it's worth mentioning that looking after our general mental health has a positive impact on our recovery journey and treatment process. Our general self-care, compassion and gratitude can help to support us in our recovery.

➡️ What does recovery mean to you, Ashley?

I have two answers to this: in short it's about living your life the way you want, how you want, when you want, regardless of any anxiety that intrusive thoughts may throw at us.

A rather mundane example of this is that after twenty years of avoiding public toilets and hours of washing compulsions after using my own, recovery for me is now being able to use toilets, public or at home, regardless of anxiety. That's not to say I don't still experience anxiety – I do when using the bathroom, but I can leave without washing my hands if necessary and the anxiety fades within moments... for me, that is recovery in action.

Does that mean I no longer have OCD? Sadly no – I still have OCD impacting on me in a few ways, but I am determined to continue working every single day of my life to challenge that, and I hope if we ever produce a second edition of this book, that I will be able to update it to say that OCD is no longer present or no longer stops me doing anything I want. That is the ultimate recovery for me.

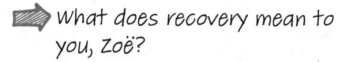

What does recovery mean to you, Zoë?

I used to believe that I would have to manage OCD every day for the rest of my life. However, over recent years my opinion has certainly changed, and that's not due to my beliefs but rather my own experiences. Recovery to me means no longer living life the way OCD wants me to, but instead doing it my way, despite sometimes needing to apply the tools I've learned in therapy, and through my journey with the charity. This doesn't mean that I am managing OCD every day, but it does mean if I feel in a vulnerable position for OCD to creep back, I feel confident in my learnings through therapy that I will stick to my guns and face off the OCD beast!

I personally feel that recovery will teach you new lessons in itself. You'll learn to recognize how far you have come, and how different your responses to the cries of OCD are.

To sum up, recovery to me is no more compulsions, no more answering to OCD's demands, but being kind and gentle with myself if I hit a bump in the road every so often. If I do slip again, I'll know what to do if that happens. I will never go back to not knowing and that itself makes me feel powerful.

FAQs

1 About OCD – The Basics
What is OCD?

What is an obsession?

What is a compulsion?

What is an OCD trigger?

Why is OCD a disorder?

Is OCD a disability?

Is OCD a mental illness?

What percentage of adults have OCD?

What is reassurance in OCD?

2 Understanding OCD
How do obsessions and compulsions reinforce each other?

What is a groinal response?

What is an OCD avoidance?

What is rumination?

Are compulsions always a problem?

Is limiting myself to just one or two compulsions enough?

What age can someone be diagnosed with OCD?

What is Thought-Action Fusion?

Does OCD run in families?

What causes OCD?

Are there types of OCD?

Why does my OCD 'theme' change?

How do I know what type of obsession someone has from their behaviours?

How do I know if I am doing something because I enjoy it or because OCD is making me?

Why can't people with OCD just stop the compulsions?

3 Debunking OCD Myths

Do only kind and sensitive people get OCD?

Does everybody have a little bit of OCD?

Do people with OCD all have spotless homes?

Why are more people suffering with OCD now?

Will an ex-sufferer be the best therapist to help me because they have experienced OCD?

Is hoarding part of OCD?

Can you have both OCD and OCPD?

Shouldn't people with OCD just laugh off OCD jokes?

Why do people with OCD get upset when OCD is trivialized?

How should we challenge OCD misuse?

Is it OK to laugh about my OCD?

4 Children and OCD

Is it my fault my child has OCD?

Does giving my child reassurance make OCD worse?

Will my child's future be severely impacted by OCD?

How do I know if the therapy my child is receiving is good therapy?

Is my child too young for treatment?

Should we tell the school?

How do we tell a sibling?

How old can a child be to formally diagnose OCD?

Can my child with OCD get help from school?

My child won't talk to me about OCD, what can I do?

How do I respond to my child's anger and frustration?

5 Lifestyle

Will my period make OCD worse?

Is it harder to date with OCD?

When should I tell a new partner about my OCD?

Does having OCD mean I will always be single?

Should I look for a partner who also has OCD?

Does exercise help with OCD?

Can people with OCD claim benefits?
Can I get help with water bills?
Will having OCD affect my travel insurance?
Do I need to tell the DVLA that I have OCD?
Can a person with a diagnosis of OCD receive social care from
a local authority?

6 Diagnosing OCD

Do online self-assessment questionnaires tell me if I have OCD
or not?
How do I get a formal diagnosis?
What should I tell the doctor/therapist?
Will OCD appear on my medical records?

7 Treatment for OCD

What is the best mediation for OCD?
Do I have to take mediation to treat OCD?
Can medication cause side-effects?
What is CBT?
What is ERP?
What is the difference between CBT and ERP?
Why do we do ERP?
What is anti-OCD?
Does hypnotherapy help?
Does EMDR help?
Does mindfulness help with OCD?
What is a hierarchy?

8 How to Access Treatment

Do you need a therapist to overcome OCD?
How do I access treatment?
Which is better – an NHS therapist or a private therapist?
Do I need a psychologist or psychiatrist?
How many therapy sessions will I need?

9 Treatment Myths

What if treatment doesn't help?

Am I treatment resistant?

Is it harder to treat older people and people who have had OCD for many years?

I was told I must wait three months for more treatment, is this true?

Should therapy only take place in the therapist's office?

Does overcoming OCD mean not having intrusive thoughts?

10 OCD Self-help

What can I do whilst on a several-month-long treatment waiting list?

What are the best books for OCD?

Will talking in a support group make my OCD worse?

Will reading OCD blogs help?

11 Working and OCD

Are people with OCD less employable?

Will OCD stop me working?

Does the doctor have to tell my employer about my OCD?

Should I tell my employer about my OCD?

Are there jobs that people with OCD are more suited for?

What are OCD reasonable adjustments for work?

I find my job makes my OCD worse – should I stop working or change jobs?

12 Life in Recovery

What should I do in recovery?

What is relapse prevention?

Does someone in recovery from OCD have to be careful not to slip into old habits?

About the Authors

About Ashley

Ashley first remembers what he now knows to be OCD symptoms when he was a teenager, which became significantly problematic around the age of 17/18. Now 49, like many adults of his generation, he went many years from first having symptoms to receiving a formal diagnosis, and does not recall exactly when his OCD first started. After being asked 'What is OCD?' by a GP in East London when he first reached out for help, Ashley was determined to try and make a difference to help others not go through the same; this book continues that work.

Born in the East Midlands, Ashley's interests include cycling around the northern slopes of the Serra de Tramuntana mountain range in Majorca and across the hills of Derbyshire, where he now lives. His other passion is supporting his beloved Nottingham Forest, where he is a season ticket holder in the upper Trent End. Ashley recently wrote that attending football, even through the difficult on-pitch period, was helpful in maintaining and lifting his mental health during difficult times.

Ashley has worked for OCD-UK since 2004 after originally being part of a team that set up the charity the previous year.

About Zoë

Zoë was approximately 8 years old when she first started to experience Obsessive-Compulsive Disorder, but it wasn't until her early 20s that the symptoms had become so unbearable she needed therapeutic help. Throughout the years, Zoë has experienced a large handful of different themes with OCD and has found them all to be as awful as each other.

Zoë started working for the OCD-UK charity in November 2019, and at this point she was in a comfortable place in her recovery journey. Since then, Zoë has progressed even further, branched out and grown into new learnings, and discovered even more information that has supported her recovery.

Acknowledgements

Gemma Blueitt

Rose Gardener

Laura Hickman

Catherine Mills

Professor Paul Salkovskis

Christina Webb

Ashley's personal acknowledgements

I have been working for OCD-UK since 2003, and in that time, I have worked with many wonderful people, volunteers, colleagues, trustees – some have been passing through, others I still work with to this day. To all of them, both people with OCD and health professionals, I want to thank you for helping, inspiring and educating me.

Special mentions to Catherine, Steve and Paul who helped me ensure OCD-UK became a reality, and who have guided and mentored me ever since.

Zoë's personal acknowledgements

I will be eternally grateful to the people in my life who have held my hand through the dark days and walked beside me during the most challenging times. To my Mum, Dad, my brother and Lee – thank you. And a big thank you to Michael – finding the 'right' therapist is invaluable, and you have provided me with the tools to stand up to OCD and take back control of my own life.